GAY HEAD
LIGHTHOUSE

GAY HEAD
LIGHTHOUSE

....

THE FIRST LIGHT ON
MARTHA'S VINEYARD

WILLIAM WATERWAY

FOREWORD BY WAYNE C. WHEELER
FOUNDER/PRESIDENT OF THE BOARD FOR THE UNITED STATES LIGHTHOUSE SOCIETY

Charleston ‖H‖ London
THE
History
PRESS

Published by The History Press
Charleston, SC 29403
www.historypress.net

First published 2014

Manufactured in the United States

ISBN 978.1.62619.406.9

Library of Congress CIP data applied for.

a
torch
red and white
to guide us through

water

churning beneath Devil's Bridge
rising, threatening our
sailors' landfall

Gay Head Light

in darkest dark
of stormy night
she reaches out
flame so bright
forever my love
illuminate truth

protect our lights
from hidden dark
working in stealth
to steal our wealth
leaving dark mark
on our future youth

dedicated to Martha's Vineyard and poetic justice
for our island's light

~~~~~~
~~~~~~~~~~~~~~~~~
~~~~~~
~~~~~~~~~~~~~~~~~

ww

CONTENTS

Contents

FOREWORD

I was delighted to learn that William Waterway had written a book about one of America's earliest light stations and also the first one I visited when a very young lad.

I summered on Martha's Vineyard with my family from the time I was seven until after I left for college, and I've returned many times since. Around 1949, my father announced he was taking my sister and me to see a lighthouse. What that was, I had no idea. My only memory of that visit was when a Coast Guard sailor assisted me up the ladder and into the lantern room, where I was dazzled and stunned by the light reflecting off the first-order Fresnel lens, an optic with over one thousand prisms. Overall, a first-order lens stands nineteen feet high and is six feet in diameter. To me, it was a very impressive experience at the time.

The Gay Head station was established in 1799, one of just twenty-two American light stations established before 1800. The lighthouse marked a dangerous and heavily used passage between the island and the mainland known as Devil's Bridge.

Although the Gay Head station has been written about or mentioned in numerous books and articles, this comprehensive work by Waterway is a welcome addition to the few scholarly works on my favorite subject. The site has a colorful and significant history. The colorful cliffs of Gay Head are unique in themselves. The station was one of the first in this country to receive a first-order Fresnel lens, and its early history includes two Indian keepers, including the first Indian principal keeper in America's history in 1922.

This is a good read and a well-researched work. It belongs in every lighthouse enthusiast's library.

WAYNE C. WHEELER
Founder/President of the Board
United States Lighthouse Society

PREFACE

This book is written in remembrance of our Gay Head Light keepers—keepers who, for little money and oftentimes as much recognition, made sacrifices and toiled long hours to ensure safe sailing for passing seafarers.

In the early 1980s, Vineyard Environmental Research Institute (VERI), an organization I founded, was given access to the Gay Head Light. It was the first time in U.S. history that a civilian organization was given a lease for an "active" aid to navigation.

In 1985, I felt honored to open the door of the hallowed brick tower that has saved so many lives. As years passed, I learned of the tragic deaths of children born to Keeper Crosby Crocker and his wife, Eliza. After publishing the Crosby family tragedy in *Martha's Vineyard Magazine*, I felt haunted. As I walked up the lighthouse stairs, I often imagined the Crosby children climbing and playing along the same steel stairs—stairs that sing and vibrate to the weight of footfalls.

With little doubt, the lightweight footfalls of the Crosby children were those of wide-eyed youths living in the moment without thought of death. I asked myself, "Who am I to walk the stairs of innocent youth, laboring keepers, curious tourists, romantic lovers, inquisitive neighbors and thankful sailors—all of whom, through time, sought something from this beckoning light?"

This is a light whose outstretched arm reaches across the waters—waters of millennia flowing through all life, through the center of our Earth and through our sky and stars. The same water that now threatens to embrace the light and drag it down into the dark depths of Devil's Bridge.

In a poetic fashion, the ocean is now seeking to reclaim the clays born within its depths. Clays fired into bricks by human hands to create a tower—a tower to hold a light to illuminate the night for sailors' sight.

A light now perched atop a crumbling cliff just beyond reach of ocean's might.

WILLIAM WATERWAY

Acknowledgements

Charles Vanderhoop Jr. — lighthouse friend born at Gay Head Light

Tabitha Dulla — editor, The History Press

Arthur Railton — editor emeritus, *Dukes County Intelligencer*

David Nathans — director, Martha's Vineyard Museum

Nathaniel Janick — librarian, Martha's Vineyard Museum

Hillary Wall — research librarian, *Martha's Vineyard Gazette*

Wayne Wheeler — founder, United States Lighthouse Society

Timothy Harrison — founder, *Lighthouse Digest*

Thomas Dresser — Martha's Vineyard historian

Sarah and Casey Oldham — my daughter and son-in-law

Kevin Marks — my brother

Christopher Decker — Tisbury printer

Cynthia Riggs — author and patron, Cleaveland House Poets

Michael and Jena King — dear friends

Peter Steel and Raven Bird — water historians

Elise Elliston — historian/neighbor

John Bitzer Jr. — past chair, Vineyard Environmental Research Institute

Jim Pickman — originator, Gay Head Light Poetry Project

Beverly Wright — chair, Save the Gay Head Light Committee

Tobias Vanderhoop — chair, Aquinnah Wampanoag Tribal Council

Bettina Washington — Aquinnah Wampanoag tribal preservation officer

Acknowledgements

Martha Vanderhoop — Save the Gay Head Light Committee, daughter of Charles Vanderhoop

Mitzi Pratt — bookbinder for the Gay Head Light Poetry Project book

Victoria Haeselbarth — historian of the Martha's Vineyard Sea Coast Defence chapter of the DAR

Ann Vanderhoop — local historian/owner of Vanderhoop Restaurant

Buddy Vanderhoop — local historian/Tomahawk Fishing Charters

Paul Schneider — editor, *Martha's Vineyard Magazine*

Betsy Mayhew — lighthouse director, Martha's Vineyard Museum

Richard Skidmore — modern-day lighthouse keeper

Joan LeLacheur — modern-day lighthouse keeper

Margaret DeWolf — widow of Nick DeWolf (photographer)

Anna Carringer — assistant curator, Martha's Vineyard Museum

Jeff Gales — United States Lighthouse Society

Aquinnah Board of Selectmen
United States Coast Guard
Martha's Vineyard Poetry Society

To the Gay Head light keeper's families—especially the Vanderhoops, Sewards, Flanderses, Smiths, Eddys, Attaquins, Grieders, Hindleys, Lamburts, Bettencourts, Luces, Pooles, Peases and many others.

And to pharologists and lovers of the Gay Head Light who appreciate what it offers to Martha's Vineyard and our world's maritime culture and history.

CHAPTER 1

LIGHTHOUSE SEDUCTION AND SALVATION

In bed—I watch her seductive light
white, white, white and red

The first record of a ship sailing the waters of Nantucket Sound between Gay Head Cliffs and the Elizabeth Islands can be found in Bartholomew Gosnold's 1602 ship journal. "[On] the four and twentieth of May," wrote the ship's journalist as they sailed away from Noman's Land, "we set sail and doubled the cape of another island next unto this, which we called Dover Cliff, and then came into a fair sound." The resemblance of the Gay Head Cliffs to England's Dover Cliff prompted the written analogy. The "fair sound" probably refers to what is known today as Vineyard Sound.

Today, the Gay Head Light vista across the cliffs is considered one of America's most treasured coastal experiences. As such, the clay cliffs are protected as a National Natural Landmark, and the lighthouse is listed on the National Register of Historic Places. Sightseers may enjoy the remarkable Gay Head experience from the "lookout" area located by the Aquinnah shops, by taking a walk along the beach below the clay cliffs or by viewing the awe-inspiring clay cliffs vista while visiting the Gay Head Light during the summer season.

The Gay Head Light, the island's first lighthouse, was located in the westernmost town of Gay Head (today's Aquinnah in 1799). It was octagonal in shape and made of wood. Over time, in addition to the Gay Head Light, there would be five other lighthouses built on

Martha's Vineyard at different locations. This unusual clustering of so many lighthouses within such a small geographical area makes Martha's Vineyard unique when compared to more than 16,900 lighthouse locations around the world.

I first visited Gay Head in the early 1970s during a trip with my college girlfriend. The architectural lines of the brick Gay Head Light intrigued me. Years later, while doing an erosion study of Martha's Vineyard, the U.S. Coast Guard (USCG) provided me with a key for storing coastal research equipment in the lighthouses. It was then that I learned that the Gay Head Light, along with two other island lights, were being considered for decommissioning.

SAVING GAY HEAD LIGHT IN THE 1980s

My first contact at the USCG properties division was with Laurie Boudreau, commander of the First Coast Guard District in Boston. Ms. Boudreau indicated that I would have to work with Congress to save the Gay Head Light from being decommissioned and possibly demolished and replaced by a skeleton tower with a strobe light. She also said, "The only way I believe you can save the lighthouse is if your organization is willing to assume the care and expense of maintaining it."

I immediately initiated contact with Massachusetts congressman Gerry Studds and Senator Ted Kennedy. As fate would deliver, Congressman Gerry Studds was recently appointed chairman of the House Committee on Merchant Marine and Fisheries and was working closely with the Lighthouse Preservation Society to save lighthouses. The timing was perfect for my proposal to arrive in Washington for saving the island's lighthouses. Congressman Studds gave his support, as did Senator Kennedy.

For the next two years, the money to save the Gay Head Light, as well as two other endangered island lights (Edgartown and East Chop), came out of my own pocket. There was a lot to learn—lobbying Washington was something new to me. Along the way, I filed a proposal with the U.S. Coast Guard. In the proposal, my nonprofit organization, Vineyard Environmental Research Institute (VERI), offered to take on the responsibility of raising funds to maintain the three lighthouses in return for access to the lights for fundraising purposes.

GERRY E. STUDDS
10TH DISTRICT, MASSACHUSETTS

WASHINGTON OFFICE:
1501 LONGWORTH HOUSE OFFICE BUILDING
WASHINGTON, DC 20515
202-225-3111

COMMITTEE:
FOREIGN AFFAIRS
MERCHANT MARINE AND
FISHERIES

CHAIRMAN:
SUBCOMMITTEE ON
COAST GUARD AND NAVIGATION

Congress of the United States
House of Representatives
Washington, DC 20515

DISTRICT OFFICES:
GREATER NEW BEDFORD
POST OFFICE BUILDING
NEW BEDFORD, MA 02740
817-999-1251

SOUTH SHORE
HANOVER COURT
193 ROCKLAND STREET
HANOVER, MA 02339
617-826-3866

CAPE AND ISLANDS
146 MAIN STREET
HYANNIS, MA 02601
617-771-0666

February 18, 1986

Dear Admiral Johanson:

I have received a letter from Mr. William E. Marks, President of the Vineyard Environmental Research Institute on Martha's Vineyard, regarding his organization's efforts to lease Coast Guard lighthouses on Martha's Vineyard. I believe that the activities of this organization -- scientific research and education on the historicity of the lighthouses -- are appropriate uses of lighthouse property, especially when the dual purpose of protecting the lights from vandalism will be served.

I understand that the Coast Guard is currently processing this leasing request, and I hope that a final agreement will soon be reached that will meet the objectives of both the Coast Guard and the Vineyard Environmental Research Institute.

With kind regards.

Sincerely,

Gerry E. Studds

Admiral Robert Johanson
Commander
First Coast Guard District
Captain John Foster Williams
  Coast Guard District
408 Atlantic Avenue
Boston, MA 02210-2209

Letter from Congressman Gerry Studds supporting VERI's historic thirty-five-year license for Gay Head, East Chop and Edgartown lights. *Author's collection.*

The organization I founded, VERI, had a board of directors made up of my friends. Even though they never contributed money, they did lend their names and psychological support. When it came time for VERI to give testimony before Congress on April 30, 1986, I asked my friend and VERI board chair John Bitzer Jr. if he would like to read VERI's testimony. John, who had a literary appreciation of lighthouses, said he would be honored to do so.

Alfred Eisenstaedt (left) and author William Waterway at a VERI lighthouse fundraiser at the Harbor View Hotel, 1986. *Photo by Mark Lovewell and courtesy of* Martha's Vineyard Gazette.

The congressional lighthouse hearing was well attended. There was testimony about saving lighthouses by many organizations and individuals, including the U.S. Lighthouse Preservation Society, the U.S. Lighthouse Society, Congressman Robert William Davis, the Maryland Historical Trust, the United States Coast Guard and others. John Bitzer spoke eloquently, and his testimony and my question-and-answer segment became part of the permanent Congressional Record. VERI's testimony at the "Hearing Before the Subcommittee on Coast Guard and Navigation of the Ninety-ninth Congress" is published toward the end of this book.

A few weeks after the congressional hearings, I was pleasantly surprised to find myself signing a thirty-five-year lighthouse lease with the U.S. government. Under the terms of the lease, VERI assumed responsibility for maintaining the grounds and structures of the Gay Head, East Chop and Edgartown lighthouses. Also, as part of the agreement, the U.S. Coast Guard would continue maintaining the lens of each lighthouse as an active aid to navigation.

This was the first time in U.S. history that control of an "active" lighthouse was transferred to a civilian organization. On a similar note, this was the first time in the history of Martha's Vineyard that control of any of its five lighthouses was in the hands of an island organization.

After receiving the lighthouse license, VERI organized a series of fundraising activities that engaged the community of Martha's Vineyard, including local supporters and celebrities such as board members Fairleigh S. Dickinson Jr.; Jonathan Mayhew, whose ancestors were the Vineyard's first European settlers; *Vineyard Gazette* co-owner Jody Reston; philanthropist Flipper Harris; Margaret K. Littlefield; actress Linda Kelsey; WHOI director Derek W. Spencer; and John F. Bitzer Jr. Speakers and performers appearing at these lighthouse events were renowned historian David McCullough; Senator Ted Kennedy; Caroline Kennedy; Edward M. Kennedy Jr.; Congressman Gerry Studds; singer/songwriter Carly Simon; Kate Taylor; Livingston Taylor; Hugh Taylor; Dennis Miller from *Saturday Night Live*; Bill Styron's wife, Rose Styron, who read one of her original lighthouse poems; U.S. Navy rear admiral Richard A. Bauman; famed photographer Alfred Eisenstaedt; comedian Steve Sweeney; and others.

The proceeds from the lighthouse benefits were applied to a major restoration of the Gay Head Light, which included emergency pointing of brick walls; removing pervasive toxic mold growing on the brick interior walls; installing new windows on the ground floor and two landing levels; replacing broken plate glass and sealing roof leaks in the lighting room; restoring the hardwood staircase rail; and sandblasting, sealing and painting the historic rusted cast-iron spiral staircase and its three-story internal metal flooring and support structure.

In 1987, with the help of information supplied by VERI, the Gay Head Light was placed on the National Register of Historic Places. This elevated the importance of the Gay Head Light while under the management of VERI through its U.S. Coast Guard license number DTCGZ71101-85-RP-007L.

LOOKING BACK—LOOKING FORWARD

Because of its rich history, the Gay Head Light is often considered the most intriguing of all Vineyard lighthouses. As I researched the light's history, I learned that Gay Head light keeper Charles W. Vanderhoop's son was living near the Gay Head Light.

CHAPTER 2

MEMORIES: CHARLES W. VANDERHOOP JR.

Lighthouse memories flooded his mind late in life
his youth, his days at sea, his family, his devoted wife

Charles W. Vanderhoop Jr. was born in the Gay Head Light's keeper's house in 1921. At the time of his birth, his father, Charles Wood Vanderhoop Sr., was principal keeper.

Charles Vanderhoop Sr. was born in 1882, the youngest son of Cummings B. and Josephine (Smalley) Vanderhoop. In 1920, he became the principal keeper at the Gay Head Light. It is estimated that between 1920 and 1933, Charles W. Vanderhoop Sr. and his assistant, Max Attaquin, hosted over 300,000 visitors at the Gay Head Light.

Before getting involved with lighthouse employment, Charles Vanderhoop Sr. and his brother, Bert, bought the Vanderhoop Restaurant from his mother and stepfather, who had built the restaurant in the late 1800s. The Vanderhoop Restaurant was located near the Gay Head Light and featured a specialty of lobster dinners. Charles sold his interest in the restaurant to his brother when Bert married.

Over the ten years I knew Charles Vanderhoop Jr. and his wife, Hatsuko, I heard many stories about the Gay Head Light, about life in the Gay Head community and about his adventures sailing across our world's oceans. Charlie and I became lighthouse friends. Like a young boy, he was enthused to once again be involved with helping to maintain and save the lighthouse he knew so well as a child.

Left: A circa 1922 photograph of Charles W. Vanderhoop Sr., the first Native American principal light keeper in U.S. history. *Courtesy Martha Vanderhoop*.

Below: Charles W. Vanderhoop Jr. (front left) gave educational lighthouse tours to island schoolchildren as part of VERI's educational outreach program. *Author's collection*.

Children waiting in line for a tour with Keeper Charley Vanderhoop Jr. *Author's collection.*

Charlie had a natural gift for telling stories and working with children. He liked meeting people, and he liked sharing his life's story. When VERI initiated a grade school program to connect our island's children with the Gay Head Light, we set up regular trips to the lighthouse. While visiting the Gay Head Light, our island's children got to meet a man who was born and raised at the light.

Charlie's father, who was born on Martha's Vineyard in 1882, attended the Gay Head School. At an early age, he joined the U.S. Life-Saving Service and, later, the U.S. Lighthouse Service. In 1912, he was the assistant keeper for one year at the Sankaty Head Light in Nantucket. In 1919, he returned to Sankaty to work as the principal keeper for one year. While serving his second term at Sankaty, Charlie's father had the distinction of being the first Native American in the history of American lighthouses to serve as a principal keeper. On a related note, Sankaty was the third light in America to receive a Fresnel lens. The lens installed at Sankaty was a second-order Fresnel.

In 1920, Charles Vanderhoop Sr. was transferred from Sankaty Head Light to the Gay Head Light as principal keeper. He served in that position until 1933.

During his tour of duty as the principal keeper at the Gay Head Light, Charles Vanderhoop Sr. and his wife, Ethel, became renowned as gracious and entertaining hosts.

In the history of the Gay Head Light, there were many keepers who served their station well. However, Charles W. Vanderhoop Sr. and Samuel H. Flanders (principal keeper from 1845 to 1849 and 1853 to 1861) stood out as superstars.

Samuel Flanders, who is sometimes referred to as Martha's Vineyard's first celebrity, was famous in his day. More information about Samuel Flanders as a Gay Head Light celebrity is explored in this book's chapter about the Fresnel lens. For anyone interested, the phenomenon of Samuel Flanders is more fully explored in *Dukes County Intelligencer* 23, no. 4 (May 1982).

As a friend of Charlie's, I learned much about his life at the Gay Head Light. What impressed me most was how he enjoyed working at the lighthouse with his father. From the way Charlie Jr. spoke, it was obvious that he and his father were more than just father and son—they were friends who worked closely as a team to keep the light operating at its best.

On a personal note, this chapter was the most challenging for me to write. As best as possible, it captures my recollections through the voice of Charlie and the stories he shared.

THE VOICE OF CHARLES W. VANDERHOOP JR.

So, I guess that's how my father became familiar with how to operate a Fresnel lens. The Fresnel at Sankaty was a second-order, and the one at Gay Head was a first-order—which means the one at Gay Head was bigger and heavier. But the mechanics to illuminate and turn the lights were pretty much the same. To turn the light, you had to crank up heavy weights attached to a cable that wrapped around a brass drum on the clockworks. All the gears on the clockworks machine were made of brass because brass doesn't rust easily. The precision of that mechanical machine was amazing.

The cable was attached to a weight that was raised and lowered through a metal tube in the middle of the lighthouse. The tube went from the watch room just below the lantern room and down to the ground floor.

On the ground floor, there was a trapdoor at the bottom of the tube. The trapdoor gave us easy access to change the weights on the end of the cable. We had to adjust the weight on the cable to keep the clockworks running

Left: The so-called clockworks that supplied weight-driven mechanical energy to turn the Fresnel lens. *Author's collection.*

Right: The weight that was cranked to the top of the tower by the clockworks. *Author's collection.*

on time to give mariners an accurate light signal. It was the weight on the bottom of the cable that gave the lens the mechanical energy to turn. We had to crank that weight from the bottom of the lighthouse up to the watch room about every four hours to keep the light turning.

I remember watching my father turn the crank to lift the weight—the weight averaged 150 pounds. We always tried to crank the weight up as fast as possible because the light signal would stop turning while we were cranking. It's important to keep the signal turning and sending its signal to ships. When I was about ten years old, I was strong enough to turn the crank and lift the weight. Cranking the weight made me feel like I accomplished something—it was an important part of the lighthouse job.

Everybody pitched in and helped. There was always something to do. We were always painting or whitewashing something or patching and painting the plaster walls that covered the inside of the light from top to bottom. We painted the oil house, the barn, the fence—there was always something to maintain or fix. I think they tore out the lathe and plaster walls that used to cover the inside of the lighthouse when they tore down the house we lived in. Of course, that was after electricity came along.

We had our own garden and cold cellar for storing food through the winter. We had corn, cranberries, various fruit jellies and eggs from our own chickens, and we had a cold cellar with about a foot of sand on the bottom for storing potatoes, beets, carrots, turnips and other root vegetables. We had barrels filled with salted fish, and we had deer meat that we would jerk, smoke or salt down. It seems like we were always busy keeping the family supplied with food. We also did a lot of canning of corn, tomatoes and beans. My mother would make a relish called piccalilli by cooking vegetables mixed with her special recipe of spices. In the middle of winter, we would open a jar of relish and have that with some meat and vegetables from the cold cellar. Everything smelled and tasted fresh like it just came out of the garden. We had a garden at the lighthouse, and we had a garden at our home after leaving the lighthouse. I have a garden in my backyard right now.

Since we never had a source of good drinking water at the lighthouse, I remember my father taking the horse and wagon up to Cook's Spring and hauling the water in barrels. Getting water was a lot of work. It took a lot of effort to lift buckets of water from the spring and pour them into the barrels. A wagonload of water makes for a heavy wagon for the horse to pull. And parts of the road from the lighthouse to the spring weren't in the best of shape—especially during the winter. The wagon lurched

Charles W. Vanderhoop Jr. also served as tour guide for adults from 1986 to 1990. *Author's collection.*

Keeper Charles W. Vanderhoop Sr. and family. Charlie Jr. is sitting on his mother's (Ethel Manning Vanderhoop) lap, Charlie's sister Beulah Vanderhoop Lee is sitting next to him and his other sister, Eloise Vanderhoop Page, is standing behind Charlie and his mother. *Courtesy Martha Vanderhoop.*

back and forth in the holes and over the bumps, and the water sloshed around and splashed out of the barrels. If it was real cold, the splashing water from the barrels would freeze on the bottom of the wagon bed and form icicles that stuck out from between boards on the bottom.

We had a cistern at the house just for storing our drinking water. The underground cistern was made out of plastered brick. It was underground so the water wouldn't freeze during winter. I would pull the wagon with the water barrels up next to the cistern, remove the cistern's wooden cover and transfer the water from the barrels into the cistern. Then we would use a hand pump in the kitchen to pump water from the cistern into the house. We also had rainwater cisterns that were filled with thousands of gallons of rainwater that ran off the roof of the keeper's house. We lived on one side of the house, and the assistant keeper, Max [Attaquin], and his family lived on the other side. Everything our two families did revolved around the job of making sure the light kept shining. My father and Max figured out who would work what hours during the night shift and who would do what during the day. When it came to taking care of the light, our two families worked as one family.

We used the rainwater mostly for cleaning the lighthouse glass, doing laundry, washing pots and dishes, watering the animals and things like that. The rainwater didn't taste too bad, but it wasn't really clean water because of the clay dust that would blow up on the roof and get washed into the cistern. And then there were the droppings from the birds that would roost on top of the house. Every once in a while, we would clean out the cisterns and remove the clay silt and algae from the inside walls. The best water for drinking was the water we got from the spring.

Because we didn't have indoor plumbing, we used chamber pots, which is a fancy word for slosh buckets like we use on fishing boats. We heated our water on the woodstove. We had two outhouses that were a short walk from the house. During the time I lived there, I remember the outhouse getting blown over a couple times by big winds.

There used to be a dock and boathouse down at Pilot's Landing about a half mile away, but that was before my father was keeper. Boatload after boatload of folks would sail from places like New Bedford, Oak Bluffs and Holmes Hole to come visit our lighthouse. Some Gay Headers would meet the boats with their oxcarts and give rides back and forth to the lighthouse. Seems like almost every family in Gay Head had a team of oxen back in those days. At the end of the dock was a place known as the Pavilion. It was a large building with a restaurant. On rainy days, people could sit in

Steamer *Martha's Vineyard*, pictured here circa 1887, transported many thousands of tourists to visit the lighthouse and cliffs. *Martha's Vineyard Museum.*

the Pavilion to get out of the rain or just take a rest before getting on the boat and sailing home. I heard they used to have bands play music on some of the steamboats. The same bands would play at the Pavilion, and people danced. Eventually, they stopped traveling to the lighthouse by steamboat. The dock got damaged by heavy seas and ice and was never repaired. At very low tide, you can still see the wooden stumps of what used to be the piles for the dock.

During the 1920s, people visited the lighthouse by traveling the roads from the down-island towns. We didn't get many boat visitors at the lighthouse—not like they used to in the old days. Occasionally, someone would sail a boat and drop anchor off of Pilot's Landing and do a beach landing in a smaller boat. It was about a half-mile hike from the beach to the lighthouse.

My father liked showing off the lighthouse to visitors. People were really interested in seeing the lighthouse and its beautiful Fresnel lens. Some weekends we would have thousands of people coming and going all day long. My father would take groups for walks up and down those lighthouse stairs. There are fifty-five stairs from the bottom of the light to the top. He even gave a tour to President Calvin Coolidge just after he left office. My father said that President Coolidge had some people with him who asked questions, but all Coolidge did was nod his head and smile once in a while. My father also gave a tour to the famous movie-star comedian Harold Lloyd.

My father did such a good job caring for the lighthouse that he received merit stars from the United States Lighthouse Service. In 1920, the first year my father was principal keeper up at Gay Head, the Lighthouse Service passed regulations for wearing uniforms. The Service required that my father and his assistant always wear their uniforms, which they had to pay for themselves. They could have their uniforms made or could order them from a catalog that provided that kind of service.

My father wore a uniform during most of the thirteen years he was at the Gay Head Light. That's why a lot of photos you see of my father—even when he is relaxing with our family—show him wearing his lighthouse uniform. He had different kinds of uniforms. The dress uniform he wore when on duty and when giving tours, and he had a regular uniform he would wear when off duty. He had a summer uniform and a heavier winter uniform. Even the hat he wore had to be made according to regulations. When he wore his white uniform, he had to wear white shoes. When he wore his navy blue uniform, he had to wear black shoes. There was a long list of rules about lighthouse keepers and their uniforms.

It took a lot of work for my mother to keep my father's uniforms clean and his dress shirts pressed with an iron. Our clothes iron, oil lamps, fuel cans and other items were supplied by the Lighthouse Depot. My father's uniforms were expensive. He wore coveralls over his uniform when repairing and oiling the chariot system that turned the Fresnel, working in the garden, cleaning the smoke stains from the prisms and lamps and washing the lighthouse windows. We cleaned the glass and prisms of the Fresnel every day and often gave the lantern room windows a quick wash.

The two families living at the lighthouse worked together to maintain the buildings and equipment in good order. Everything was kept clean and organized. Sometimes the lighthouse inspector for our district would stop by unannounced. Our lighthouse always passed inspection and received good ratings. Before my father retired, he received a blue star pin from the United States Lighthouse Service.

The discipline of the Lighthouse Service was very strict. If a keeper was found out of uniform, he could be fined. If a keeper was found intoxicated, it was grounds for immediate dismissal, and they would have to leave the keeper's house. Of course, the biggest offense a keeper could ever commit was to allow the light to go out during the night. On the rare occasion this happened in other parts of the country, the keeper was fired on the spot. He was discharged for poor conduct and lost all retirement benefits.

Every morning, just before sunrise, it was important to shut off the kerosene oil to the lantern wick in the lighting room, lock down the weights and pull down the spring roll curtains around the Fresnel to protect it from the sun. The magnifying lens of the Fresnel could capture the rays of the sun and heat up and damage the lens.

We always kept a five-gallon can of oil up in the watch room. The oil shed was a short walk to the lighthouse. Every day, we had to carry cans of kerosene from the oil shed up to the watch room. My father was strong—he could carry two five-gallon cans of oil up those stairs at the same time.

At the top of the lighthouse, the lamp inside the lens had to be kept filled with oil. We had to watch the oil levels in the lamp all night.

Besides keeping the oil lamp chimney clean and the lens clean, we also had to keep the outside windows of the lantern room clean. That meant going outside on the balcony in all kinds of weather and scraping off any snow or ice. During a dark storm, we had to keep the light burning twenty-four hours a day.

We were always careful working with fuel and fire. The oil house was separate from the lighthouse. We had a woodstove in the clock room in the winter and woodstoves in the keeper's house. We were required to keep red buckets filled with water and sand to put out fires. These buckets were located in handy places in the lighthouse and the keeper's house.

My father liked archaeology and was always climbing and digging around in the clay looking for fossils. His greatest find was a huge petrified Megalodon tooth that was millions of years old. Do you know what a

Megalodon is? It is a huge shark. That tooth is one of my most prized possessions from my father. The Megalodon shark was up to sixty feet long and was the top predator of the ocean's food chain. Finding that big shark's tooth was a big deal. There was a Harvard professor named Dr. Parker who would bring students down to the lighthouse every summer to see my father's Megalodon tooth. Then the students would go out and dig all day around the cliffs for fossils.

My family lived at the Gay Head Light for thirteen years. When we left the lighthouse, we moved a short distance up the road. If I remember correctly, in addition to free housing, the Lighthouse Service provided a fuel allowance to help us pay for the wood or peat we used to heat our home and the lighthouse. For heat in the main living area of our house, we had a Magee Grand woodstove. You always remember a woodstove. It's like an old friend. It is a source of memories filled with warmth and comfort—especially during long winter nights when the wind is howling. In the lighthouse clock room, just below the lantern room, we used a Magee Beacon woodstove to help us keep warm through night watches. Every fall, when it started to get cold, we would carry the Magee Beacon stove up into the clock room. When warm weather came in the spring, we would remove the woodstove and store it away in the barn. This allowed for more room in the watch room when tourists came to visit during the warm season.

My father retired in 1933 because he started having leg problems. I guess all those trips up and down the lighthouse stairs took their toll. After my father retired, he felt he was owed retirement benefits that he never received. At first, he asked the Lighthouse Service to pay him what he was owed. After quite a few years went by, he stopped talking and took action. My father legally challenged the United States of America and won. Imagine that! The federal government even passed an "Act" in my father's name when they paid him.

A year before they electrified the Gay Head Light and removed the Fresnel, there was quite a bit of controversy. Folks in Gay Head wanted the Fresnel to stay in town. After everything settled in 1952, the Fresnel lens was moved from the lighthouse to the Dukes County Historical Society in Edgartown. There was a dedication ceremony for the Fresnel at its new location, and they had my father light the lens. My father was a member of the society as well as several other organizations. He even served a term as sheriff. I remember when he lit the Fresnel lens at its new location—he got all dressed up in his best keeper's uniform. It was a nice way for the island to honor my father's years of service.

I believe my years as a boy watching ships sail by the lighthouse gave me the idea of becoming a ship captain. Besides that, I was always meeting people from all over the world who visited the lighthouse. After high school, I trained to become a merchant marine. After graduating from the Merchant Marine Officer Training Center in 1943, I served by sailing Liberty ships during World War II in the Atlantic and Pacific. Liberty ships were about 450 feet long and could carry up to ten thousand tons. The Merchant Marines was a group of sailors that kept our military supplied as we fought the war. It was dangerous work. The Merchant Marines suffered the highest death rate of any branch of service. When I was sailing Liberty ships, sometimes all we had for navigation was a compass and a sextant. I was always figuring out where our ship was in the ocean to keep us on a course.

When the war was over, I got my unlimited master's license to captain large cargo ships. Do you know what an "unlimited master's license" is? It's a license that allows you to captain vessels of unlimited tonnage across all of the oceans of the world, and it is considered the highest-level license for a ship captain. Sailing big ships is a lot of responsibility—that's why it was important for me to know where coastal landmarks, especially lighthouses, were located. I had to read charts and know where lighthouses were located along the coasts of different countries. After crossing the ocean in a big ship, it was always a welcome site to see the beam of a lighthouse reaching out across the water. I've lost count of the lighthouses in other countries that helped to guide my ships to a safe landfall.

Besides sailing large cargo vessels, I also captained a research ship out of the University of Rhode Island named the Trident. *It was a research vessel with rooms jam-packed with scientific equipment. I visited the Galapagos many times with research scientists. The wildlife on those islands is so beautiful it would bring tears to your eyes.*

I eventually began to think of settling down. After meeting and marrying Hatsuko in 1953 and having our two children, Charlie and Martha, my life changed. I met Hatsuko in Japan during one of my shipping jobs. She's very beautiful. We always get along. Sometimes she likes making fun of me. I've lost track of the times she's said, "Charlie! Charlie! You bad Charlie, behave yourself!" And then we share a big laugh. Hatsuko means "first daughter" because she was the first daughter born into her family. Hatsuko did a good job raising Charlie Boy and Martha. Once in a while, I'll bring Hatsuko's family to visit us here on the Vineyard. They think visiting our island is like taking a vacation to some kind of paradise. Hatsuko's family never really forgave me for taking her away.

In the late 1950s, I tried commercial fishing for a while—had two boats. My favorite was the Gertrude D. *One day I fell into the rigging and got injured pretty bad. So when I got better, I decided to go back to sailing merchant marine vessels. It was a tour of duty that took me to ports in Asia, India and Africa. I've lost track of all the countries I've sailed to. I figure I've sailed around the world at least thirty-seven times.*

In the early '70s, Hatsuko and I opened our gift shop up on the cliffs. We named it the Hatmarcha Shop. Today, when I do scrimshaw while sitting in the corner of our shop, I find inspiration from my boyhood days while living at the Gay Head Light. I also find inspiration from the places I've seen and from my being out to sea as captain of so many different ships.

At this time in my life, I see how some things come around full circle. I am now helping out as a lighthouse keeper at the Gay Head Light—the lighthouse where I was born. Imagine that! I love spending time talking with children from our island schools about the Gay Head Light. Our island's schools do a good job teaching our kids about lighthouses. They do art projects, poetry projects, history projects—all kinds of projects about our lighthouses. It's amazing the number of good questions those kids ask me when they come up and visit me at my lighthouse.

***

Author's note: During World War II, Charles Vanderhoop Jr. served aboard Liberty supply ships as part of the North Atlantic convoy to Murmansk, Russia. While serving in the U.S. Coast Guard Merchant Marines, he was awarded the Merchant Marine Emblem, the Atlantic War Zone Bar, the Mediterranean-Middle East War Zone Bar and the Pacific War Zone Bar.

PLASTER WALLS INSIDE THE GAY HEAD LIGHT

Charles Vanderhoop Jr.'s mentioning to me that the inside of the Gay Head Light once had walls covered with plaster came as a surprise. In my years of involvement with the Gay Head Light, this was the first time I had heard this fact

Subsequently, I researched U.S. Lighthouse Service documents produced during the years Charles W. Vanderhoop Sr. was the principal keeper—from 1920 to 1933. While doing so, I found documentation of an official inspection report made of the Gay Head Light. This March 13, 1922 document was signed off by George W. Eaton, superintendent of the U.S. Lighthouse Service. Under the heading "Description of Light Station" is the following handwritten notation: "Tower lathed and plastered on inside, 12-inch hollow cast column in center. Parapet brick lathed and plastered on inside."

This record confirms Charles Vanderhoop Jr.'s statement that the walls inside the Gay Head Light were once covered with plaster. It is possible that when the Gay Head Light was first built in 1854–56, it was constructed with interior walls covered with plaster. This would have made the interior of the lighthouse warmer during the winter and less likely to have water and moisture infiltration.

At this time, it is estimated that the interior lathe and plaster walls of the lighthouse were removed in the late early 1960s when the keeper's house was demolished. The 1963 photograph in Chapter 19 of this book shows what appears to be a pile of white plaster that was thrown out from the window above.

CHARLES W. VANDERHOOP SR.–LITIGATION WITH THE UNITED STATES OF AMERICA

Charles Vanderhoop Jr. refers to his father taking the United States of America to court for retirement pay. My research confirmed that there was settlement of a case between Charles W. Vanderhoop Sr. and the United States of America. This case is published in the U.S. Government Printing Office records as follows:

AN ACT
For the relief of Charles W. Vanderhoop

October 31, 1951 [H.R. 2546] *Private Law 410, Chapter 659*

Be it enacted by the Senate and House of Representatives of the United States of America in Congress assembled, That the Secretary of the Treasury be, and he is hereby, authorized and directed to pay, out of any money in the Treasury not otherwise appropriated, the sum of $639.39 to

Charles W. Vanderhoop, of Gay Head, Massachusetts, in full settlement of all claims against the United States for adjustment of retirement pay for the period January 1, 1933, to December 29, 1937, as a retired employee of the former Lighthouse Service of the Coast Guard: Provided, That no part of the amount appropriated in this Act in excess of 10 per centum thereof shall be paid or delivered to or received by any agent or attorney on account of services rendered in connection with this claim, and the same shall be unlawful, any contract to the contrary notwithstanding. Any person violating the provisions of this Act shall be deemed guilty of a misdemeanor and upon conviction thereof shall be fined in any sum not exceeding $1,000.

Approved October 31, 1951.

CHAPTER 3

WHALING, SHIPPING COMMERCE AND DEVIL'S BRIDGE = GAY HEAD LIGHT

America's first oil boom—was found floating inside living whales
it gave life to our island economy—for whales it beckoned doom

WHALES A PLENTY SURROUNDING MARTHA'S VINEYARD

When Captain John Smith passed through Vineyard Sound in 1614, he wrote, "Mighty whales spewing up water like the smoke of a chimney, and making the sea about them white and hoary."

The harvesting of whale oil for use in lanterns and as a lubricant was a natural transfer of knowledge by colonists. Settlers were already familiar with the production of tallow oil from animal fat. Tallow was used to make candles, soap and lubricants, as well as a dressing for preserving and softening leather. The use of harvested whale oil might have been learned from Native Americans or organically evolved as part of colonial culture. Regardless, it did not take long before colonists discovered the superior properties of whale oil.

By 1796, the sea around Cape Cod and the islands were filled with sailing vessels. The sails of hundreds of ships were visible from the Vineyard's beaches—ships from countries around the globe with holds filled with cargo to fuel the commerce of international trade. And perhaps the largest and most majestic of all the ships gracing the sea were the square-rigged whale ships originating from Martha's Vineyard, Nantucket and New Bedford.

At various times, perhaps during nights graced by a full moon with favorable winds, these large ships navigated through the treacherously narrow and rock-strewn passage between Gay Head and the Elizabeth Islands.

For more than a century, between 1750 and 1850, the global headquarters of the spermaceti whale oil and candle-making industries were located on Nantucket. At the time, spermaceti whale oil was considered the highest-quality, most expensive most sought-after oil on the market.

Prior to whale oil, most people illuminated their homes with tallow candles molded from beef or mutton fat. For people too poor to avail themselves of homemade tallow candles, the "tallow dip"—a strip of burning cloth in a saucer of tallow grease—was the dirty, smelly alternative.

NANTUCKET'S SPERMACETI WHALE OIL CANDLE FACTORIES

To get a perspective of the size of Nantucket's lucrative spermaceti candle-making industry, all one has to do is visit today's Nantucket's Whaling Museum. The building occupied by today's whaling museum was once the home of one such candle-making factory.

In the early 1800s, Nantucket's thirty-five spermaceti candle-making factories were exporting candles around the globe. Far superior to animal tallow or beeswax, spermaceti oil's ability to produce a bright, smokeless flame made it a fuel source that was second to none—a quality that soon led to intense demand. Spermaceti candles burned longer and brighter and had a cleaner smell than other candles. As a result, wealthy people in America, England and France preferred spermaceti candles from Nantucket. In fact, the spermaceti candle "bright-light" phenomenon was so unique that it became the basis for a new light standard: the "lumen." It was for these reasons that sperm whale oil was eventually specified by the U.S. Lighthouse Establishment as the only oil permitted in America's lighthouses.

But as the tides of fortune always change, Nantucket's early success in the candle business was eventually equaled and possibly eclipsed by a whale oil candle-making factory on Martha's Vineyard.

WORLD'S LARGEST WHALE OIL CANDLE FACTORY ON MARTHA'S VINEYARD

Historian Janet Van Tassel wrote the following in *The Intelligencer* in November 1975:

> *In 1835, Josiah Gorham and Benjamin Barney, both of Nantucket, purchased the wharf store and large tract of land owned by Charles Smith and John Holmes and constructed an oil refinery and candleworks on the lot. Gorham bought his partner's share of the business in November 1835 and in May 1836 sold half of the company's holding to Daniel Fisher, a physician of considerable wealth and influence. In 1838, Dr. Fisher purchased the remainder of the industry, including the wharf and store, for $6,500.*

Fisher modernized the oil refinery and candle-making operation and expanded the storage capacity for whale oil. The large whale oil storage warehouse allowed Fisher to purchase oil at a market discount in large quantities. Fisher's oil storage warehouse was so large that it was colloquially known as "Dr. Fisher's Fort." According to Van Tassel, "In 1850, Dr. Fisher's candle factory produced candles, refined oil, and pressings worth $284,370 and had $257,000 worth of whale oil in stock."

By 1860, Dr. Fisher's whale oil candle-making factory was considered the largest of its kind in the world.

THE GOLDEN AGE OF WHALING

For a variety of reasons—mostly importantly their proximity to whale migration patterns—Nantucket, Martha's Vineyard, Provincetown and New Bedford evolved into the whale oil mining capitals of the world. By the late 1700s and early 1800s, whalers from these towns were ranked as the world's leaders. With whale oil prices steadily climbing and the rest of the country's economy struggling, these Massachusetts villages soon became the wealthiest in the country. On any given year in the mid-1800s, more than seven hundred whaling ships were sailing the world's oceans—four hundred of these ships called New Bedford their homeport. Wealthy whaling captains built large houses in the best neighborhoods, and New Bedford became known as "The City that Lit the World."

The first whaling ship of record that sailed from Martha's Vineyard was the schooner *Lydia*, with Peter Pease as master. The *Lydia* left Edgartown for a voyage to Davis Straits in 1765. By 1846, the Vineyard town of Edgartown had nineteen whaling vessels plying the world's oceans, with up to fifty ships being fitted out at one time. In those days, the port of Edgartown was one of the most important on the coast. Ships from all parts of the world came to Edgartown for clearance papers and to pay duties on cargoes. Most importantly, ships often weighed anchor at Edgartown to take on provisions of food, goods and water.

As whale ships became larger, Nantucket's shallow harbor became inadequate. The protected deepwater ports of Edgartown and Vineyard Haven's became ideal harbors for large whale ships to take on provisions, undergo repairs and sell goods.

Downtown Edgartown markets capitalizing on the whaling boom included food markets selling locally grown grains, vegetables, meat, cheese, honey and jellies; bakery shops; coppersmiths (aka redsmiths); coopers, who made wooden barrels, casks and buckets; tinsmiths (aka whitesmiths); blacksmiths; clothing shops selling homemade sweaters, socks, gloves, coats and oilskin rain gear; chandlers buying whale oil to manufacture candles they then sold to whalers and commercial markets; shipwrights who built and repaired ships; sailmakers; restaurants; bars; rooming houses; barber shops (which also did bloodletting); and livery stables for horses, oxen and the carts and wagons they pulled.

Downtown Edgartown experienced a building boom with expansive captain houses being built along streets overlooking the harbor. The Whaling Church was built in 1843 and survives as one of the finest examples of Greek Revival architecture.

Island farms and saltworks flourished as they found a steady and growing demand for their salt, meat, vegetables, grains, flour, wool and milk byproducts. As published in my 1980 book, *The History of Wind-Power on Martha's Vineyard*, by 1861, there were wind-powered solar saltworks in almost every Cape Cod and island town producing over 1 million bushels of salt a year.

According to Janet Van Tassel's report on island farm production:

> *There were 265 farms on the Vineyard in 1850—79 in Edgartown, 90 in Tisbury and 96 in Chilmark—which produced a total of 12,000*

bushels of corn, nearly 10,000 bushels of potatoes, 3,515 bushels of oats, 2,075 bushels of rye and lesser quantities of barley, peas, and beans… Chilmark produced nearly half of the island's 23,147 pounds of butter.

Most importantly, Martha's Vineyard provided safe harbors to replenish the water reserves of seagoing vessels. Grafton Norton, a successful Edgartown entrepreneur who built a large house overlooking Collin's Beach, set up a lucrative business for selling spring water to ships at Collin's Wharf.

GAY HEAD'S FIRST LIGHTHOUSE

After Grey's Raid of 1778, and through the postwar 1790s, the resilient farmers on Martha's Vineyard retrenched as they once again established significant herds of sheep, cows and oxen. At the same time, there was a rapid increase in demand for whale oil candles, spring water and island farm products to supply fleets of ships.

Due to the growing success of whaling, New Bedford, the Cape and the islands soon became a shipping hub for international commerce. With this success came a large number of ships sailing the hazardous passage between Gay Head and the Elizabeth Islands.

In the late 1700s, wealthy Nantucket whaling captains and commercial shippers wielded considerable influence in the state of Massachusetts and in Washington, D.C. As a result, Massachusetts state senator Peleg Coffin stepped forward in 1796 and petitioned the newly formed federal government to build a lighthouse atop the Gay Head Cliffs.

The Gay Head Cliffs promontory was selected because of its height and strategic location overlooking two dangerous sections. One was Devil's Bridge, jutting out into the ocean from below the cliffs, and the other was the Sow and Pigs Reef, located off the west end of Cuttyhunk Island. The hidden dangers these two hazards presented was further exacerbated by the bones and rigging of sunken shipwrecks strewn amongst the submerged rocks and shoals. These hazards to ship navigation were multiplied by the ever-increasing number of sailing vessels traversing the area.

THE

History
PRESS

Enclosed you will find a review of our newest title. If you would like to get in touch with the author or need further information, please contact Sarah Falter. Send any links or hard copy reviews to the contact below as well.

Many thanks,

Sarah Falter, Publicity
THE HISTORY PRESS
645 Meeting Street. Suite 200
Charleston, SC 29403
843.577.5971, ext 227
sarah.falter@historypress.net

BEN FRANKLIN'S GULF STREAM CHART

As documented in my 2005 *Water Encyclopedia* essay published by John Wiley & Sons entitled "Ben Franklin's Gulf Stream," the rapid escalation of commercial vessels sailing the Massachusetts coast was facilitated by Benjamin Franklin's chart of the Gulf Stream. When Franklin published his navigational chart in 1769, he included directions as to how to sail at top speed on the transatlantic waterway between Europe and North America. Navigating the Gulf Stream according to Franklin's directions saved weeks of sailing time at sea. This was a significant factor in helping ships from Europe and America exchange and deliver goods for commerce, which, in turn, increased the shipping traffic passing by Devil's Bridge.

SHIPPING TRAFFIC IN THE LATE 1700s

Documentation of shipping traffic sailing the late eighteenth-century waters surrounding Martha's Vineyard is sparse. However, various records provide us with a degree of insight. One record from 1801 documents the first visual telegraph system in the United States. This system was invented by Jonathan Grout of Massachusetts and had one of its signal towers on the Martha's Vineyard promontory known as East Chop. This optical telegraph system was designed and built by Grout to span the seventy miles between Boston and Martha's Vineyard. The system was modeled after the 1792 French optical telegraph system that stretched for a distance of three thousand miles. Grout's telegraph signal towers were built on hills running from Boston, down the South Shore and across Cape Cod to Woods Hole. Each telegraph tower had a high-powered spyglass for viewing signals of other towers and for assessing and transmitting shipping news. Two men usually manned each tower from daybreak to nightfall.

The signal towers were capable of carrying messages between East Chop and Boston in ten minutes. The system also allowed for communication between the telegraph towers and ships. This communication gave American owners the option of redeploying their ships to more southerly Atlantic ports, where their cargoes might fetch higher prices. Such redeployment also allowed ships to bypass the hazardous voyage around Cape Cod to Boston. Eventually, the station at East Chop was named Telegraph Hill.

Reference to the shipping traffic sailing past Gay Head in the 1800s can also be found in a February 1939 newspaper article. The provenance of this article is from a Ms. Nancie Flanders Buell, whose ancestor Samuel Flanders was a keeper at the Gay Head Light. The article refers to ninety thousand vessels passing by the lighthouse:

> *Voyagers from abroad who made the long pilgrimage often wrote their impressions. The most notable essay of the sort is undoubtedly that contributed to* Harper's *in 1860, under the pen name of Porte Crayon. The writer was General David H. Strother, and he sketched as he went. Through his eyes the present generation may see Samuel Flanders and the Light as he kept it so many years ago.*
>
> *Another visitor to the Light in 1860 recorded that Mr. Flanders was "as faithful and as conscientious a public officer as ever drew a quarter's salary." Ninety thousand vessels passed Gay Head that year on their way through Vineyard Sound. One who went to see the Gay Head Light in 1848 wrote of "our good friend Flanders of the light-house" who acted as guide in a tour of the cliffs. In 1847, one of the literary visitors reported: "After a little delay you will find yourself quietly seated either at the residence of Mr. Flanders, the gentlemanly and polite keeper of the light, or, if you choose, with our Indian friend, Mr. Thomas Cooper, who never turns one away from his house."*
>
> *Mr. Flanders was keeper for many years, being succeeded at last by the late Ichabod N. Luce. The hospitality he showed so many visitors lives long after him on the printed page.*

On a similar note, the mid-1800s was a time when Vineyard Sound was recognized as the second-busiest waterway in the world—the English Channel being first. In the late nineteenth century, the number of sailing vessels passing the Gay Head Cliffs was reported in *Nason and Varney's Massachusetts Gazetteer*. The *Gazetteer*, which was published in 1890, reported an estimated eighty thousand vessels passing by the Gay Head Cliffs on an annual basis. The volume of vessels sailing the passage between Gay Head and the Elizabeths would, at times, fill Vineyard Sound with a zigzagging collage of white canvasses.

Considering that optimal travel conditions across the Atlantic Ocean occurred during certain months, the "rush hour" of sailing vessels passing Gay Head might have reached 200 to 350 ships per day. Not only was seasonal weather a factor—so, too, was the time of day. Prior to the installation of the

Gay Head Lighthouse, ships probably dropped anchor in safe waters and waited until daylight to navigate the narrow and hazardous passage between Devil's Bridge and the Elizabeth Islands.

MARTHA'S VINEYARD'S FIRST LIGHTHOUSE

In 1796, Senator Coffin's request to build the Gay Head Lighthouse landed on the desk of Alexander Hamilton, who was serving as secretary of the treasury. After due diligence, Hamilton requested $5,750 from Congress. On July 16, 1798, Congress voted and approved Hamilton's request. This approval occurred during the presidency of John Adams and was published in the Congressional Record:

> *Approved, July 16, 1798. Chap. [95.] An act for erecting a light-house at Gay Head, on Martha's Vineyard, and for other purposes.*

> *§ 1. Be it enacted, &c. That as soon as the jurisdiction of such land at Gay Head, on the western point of Martha's Vineyard, in the state of Massachusetts, as the president of the United States shall deem sufficient, and most proper for the accommodation of a light-house, shall have been ceded to the United States, it shall be the duty of the secretary of the treasury to provide, by contract, which shall be approved by the president, for building a light-house thereon, and for furnishing the same with all necessary supplies; and also, to agree for the salaries and wages of the person or persons who may be appointed by the president for the superintendence of the same; and the president is hereby authorized to make the said appointment.*

In 1799, the Commonwealth of Massachusetts deeded two acres and four rods to the federal government for the purpose of building a lighthouse overlooking the clay cliffs and Devil's Bridge. During the same year, President John Adams approved a contract with Martin Lincoln of Hingham, Massachusetts, to build the forty-seven-foot octagonal wooden Gay Head Lighthouse with a light room.

This first lighthouse tower on Martha's Vineyard was to be built out of wood on top of a stone base. Housing for a lighthouse keeper and his family was specified as a seventeen- by twenty-six-foot wooden house with a cellar. Also to be constructed on the site was a whale oil storage building and various other wooden outbuildings.

After three years of politicking and planning, all elements for the construction of the first Gay Head Lighthouse were finally in place. The next challenge was to build the lighthouse and set up a functional homestead for a lighthouse keeper and his family. Never before in history had anyone in America built a lighthouse and keeper's homestead on top of a clay cliff promontory. And as everyone was to discover, this was easier said than done.

However, the necessity of constructing a "landfall light" at the remote Gay Head outpost was deemed crucial for safely guiding ships through the hazardous channel. Thus, we learn the importance of the Gay Head Light as an aid to navigation known as a landfall light—so called because when sailing at night, the light from such a remote coastal lighthouse was often the first sign to sailors that land was near.

CHAPTER 4

BUILDING THE WOODEN
GAY HEAD LIGHTHOUSE

A light we must erect—above on our island's clay cliff promontory
dangerous Devil's Bridge lies in wait—thousands of ships we must protect

G ay Head's 1799 wooden octagonal lighthouse is illustrated in two separate black-and-white woodcut prints from the early 1800s. These two illustrations of our island's 1799 Gay Head Lighthouse were probably rendered *en plein air* by the artists.

A color woodcut of the 1799 lighthouse was created around 1823 by a Mrs. Hitchcock. Mrs. Hitchcock was the wife of the renowned "father of geology," Edward Hitchcock. Hitchcock was intrigued by the island's clay cliffs and made several trips to Martha's Vineyard between 1823 and 1841. In 1841, he published his book, *Final Report on the Geology of Massachusetts*. A section of Hitchcock's 1841 book about the geology at Gay Head contains his wife's color illustration of the Gay Head Cliffs and its 1799 lighthouse. This illustration represents the first color representation of the clay cliffs in recorded history. Since only a limited number of Hitchcock's books were printed, it is assumed that each color plate in each book was hand-painted.

On page 275 of his book, Hitchcock writes about the Gay Head Cliffs and its 1799 wooden lighthouse:

> *The most interesting spot on Martha's Vineyard is Gay Head, which constitutes the western extremity of this island and consists of clays and sand of various colors. It's height cannot be more than 150 feet, yet it's*

A circa 1839 woodcut showing the 1799 octagonal wooden light, keeper's house and barn. *Author's collection.*

A circa 1800 woodcut showing the 1799 octagonal wooden light and outbuildings. *Author's collection.*

variegated aspect and the richness of its colors render it a striking and even splendid object when seen from the ocean. The clays are red, blue and white; the sands, white and yellow; and the lignite, black; and each of these substances is abundant enough to be seen several miles distant, arranged in general in inclined strata; though from being unequally worn away, apparently mixed without much order. The top of the cliff is crowned by a light house, which commands an extensive prospect. Scarcely a tree is to be seen on this part of the island. It is owned and inhabited by the descendants of the Indian tribes that once possessed the whole island. It will be seen in a subsequent part of my Report, that this spot possesses peculiar attractions for the geologist and mineralogist.

I have felt quite desirous of obtaining a good drawing of Gay Head, as seen from the ocean, but have never been accompanied thither by an artist except once; and then the wind was too powerful to allow putting off in an open boat. All, therefore, that could be done, was to take an oblique view of the cliff, as seen from a high bluff near its southern part, which advances several rods beyond the general surface. Fig. 30 exhibits the northern and greater part of the Head, with the light-house, and beyond this on the right, an Indian school house; and still more distant, cliffs in Chilmark. While on the left, beyond the water, are seen some of the Elizabeth Islands and a part of Falmouth. Every lover of natural scenery would be delighted to visit this spot. There is nothing to compare with it in New England, and probably not in this country. It corresponds well with the cliffs of the Isle of Wright on the English Coast.

The accuracy of Hitchcock's description of the Gay Head Cliffs, coupled with his wife's woodcut, represent an early form of photojournalism and serve as an accurate illustration of the lighthouse and keeper's house.

In June 1799, the ten-year-old U.S. Lighthouse Establishment published its specifications for bids to build the first lighthouse on Martha's Vineyard. The two woodcuts mentioned above illustrate from afar how two different artists interpreted the appearance of the 1799 Gay Head Light. There are no photographs documenting the wooden 1799 lighthouse.

Perhaps the only "real" picture we can capture of Gay Head's first light is one we fashion in our mind's eye. The specifications to build the lighthouse were published in 1799 by the appointed Gay Head Light project supervisor, Edward Pope, collector, New Bedford. Pope published the Gay Head Lighthouse specifications on May 20, 1799, for the purpose of soliciting bids.

The bid specifications also called for a keeper's dwelling to be constructed. The interior of the house was to contain a parlor, kitchen and bedroom. Heating of the keeper's home was to be provided by two wood fireplaces and an oven. Also to be constructed near the keeper's house was a fifteen-square-foot barn.

To further help our mind's eye perceive the appearance of the 1799 Gay Head Lighthouse, I contacted architect Patrick Ahearn. I explained to Patrick the lack of drawings depicting the 1799 Gay Head Lighthouse and asked him if he could do a drawing based on the 1799 bid specifications. As a result, Patrick created a drawing of the 1799 wooden Gay Head Lighthouse. Thanks to this drawing, we have an accurate illustration of the first lighthouse constructed at Gay Head.

In the fall of 1799, our U.S. Congress chose Chilmark resident Ebenezer Skiff (age forty-nine) as the island's first principal keeper at the Gay Head Lighthouse. According to Martha's Vineyard historian Arthur Railton, Ebenezer Skiff, a Chilmark resident, "was a sometimes teacher and lawyer… His family was from Sandwich, and he married a girl from Plymouth."

In a letter dated October 3, 1799, General Benjamin Lincoln, whose son built the lighthouse, sent Ebenezer Skiff a letter:

> *I am informed by the President* [John Adams] *of the United States that he has appointed you keeper of the Light House on Gay Head; am requested to inform you that if you accept the appointment, you must live in the house built for the keeper of the Light, and not deputise any person to keep it under you, and also that you must not become a retailer of ardent spirits, for many people have informed him that a measure of this kind would destroy the Indians. Whether they are supplied or not by you, if supplied they must be ruined; if not supplied, it would produce such discontent as to destroy their present quiet and happiness. These are conditions which will always be annexed to the appointment. I am your obedient servant, B. Lincoln.*

According to the conditions stated in this letter, it appears as though Skiff was not allowed to have an assistant lighthouse keeper. Even though the tower was only 47 feet tall, due to the elevation of the cliffs, the focal plane of the light was 160 feet above the level of the sea.

On November 18, 1799, Ebenezer Skiff put a flame to wicks inside the spider lamp located in the tower's lighting room, thereby officially illuminating the Gay Head Light for the first time as an aid to navigation.

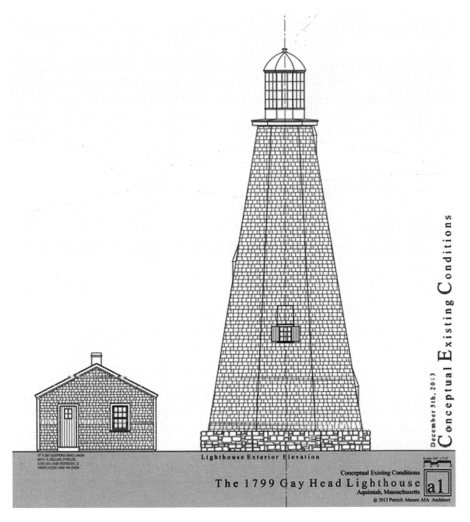

Patrick Ahearn's architectural drawing based on the 1799 lighthouse bid specifications. *Courtesy Patrick Ahearn.*

The first light at Gay Head Lighthouse was a spider lamp with wicks that absorbed fuel from a pool of sperm whale oil. Spider lamps were the principal source of light in U.S. lighthouses in the late eighteenth and early nineteenth centuries. They were stationary lights that consisted of a pan of oil with a solid system of four wicks. Spider lamps were first used at Boston Light in 1790 and were used in most lighthouses until 1812. Spider lamps were known to produce fumes that burned the keeper's eyes and obscured the light's glass with an oily smudge.

The original Gay Head Light signal was a white flash that, according to Charles Banks, "was produced by fourteen lamps burning sperm oil, and it is part of tradition of the place that there was quite as much smoke as flame resulting from the combustion of this illuminant. The keeper was often obliged to wear a veil while in the tower, and the cleansing of the smudge on the glass lantern was no small part of his job." The "veil" that Banks refers to was a piece of cloth that covered the keeper's nose and mouth to protect from inhaling smoke.

Upon its illumination, the first light from the 1799 Gay Head Lighthouse would forever change the history of Gay Head, the island of Martha's Vineyard and the world's maritime navigation of Nantucket Sound and Vineyard Sound.

CHAPTER 5

1799: TRIALS AND TRIBULATIONS
OF A LIGHT KEEPER

Life of a light keeper was tediously hard—long hours, little pay
he and family cared for the light through the night, through the day

EBENEZER SKIFF'S STARTING SALARY WAS $200 PER YEAR

After a few years as keeper of the Gay Head Light, Ebenezer Skiff realized the job of keeping the sperm oil–fired light was more labor intensive than anticipated. According to Charles Banks, the upper levels of the light were reached by climbing ladders. There was also the challenge of keeping the lantern glass clean of airborne deposits of clay particles from the nearby cliffs. After a few years of service, Ebenezer Skiff gathered the courage to write a letter requesting a pay increase to Albert Gallatin, secretary of the treasury, on October 25, 1805.

Secretary of the Treasury Gallatin reviewed Ebenezer's letter and saw the merit of Keeper Skiff's request for a pay increase. In the fall of 1805, President Thomas Jefferson increased Keeper Skiff's annual salary from $200 to $250. Skiff served as the Gay Head Light principal keeper for twenty-nine years (1799–1828). Between 1805 and 1828, Skiff received one additional $50 raise. Sometime between the years of 1810 and 1812, Keeper Skiff oversaw the replacement of the original spider lighthouse optics by ten new Lewis patent lamps. During the testing phase of these lamps, they proved to burn brighter while using about half the oil required by spider lamps.

In 1820, the spring near the Gay Head Light went dry, requiring Skiff to submit a request for a cart and casks to use in fetching water from a distant spring. Stephen Pleasonton, fifth auditor at the treasury, asked Skiff to provide a budget for the cart and casks. Upon receipt of the cost, Pleasonton authorized Skiff "to procure a pair of wheels and water casks for the use of the Keeper of Gayhead [*sic*] Light House, provided the expense shall not exceed the sum you state, viz., fifty dollars."

In 1823, Skiff sent a request to Pleasonton requesting funds to add a room to the house because there was no room "suitable for a chamber in case of sickness." Pleasonton approved Skiff's request as long as the cost did not exceed $500.

In January 1828, Ebenezer Skiff was seventy-eight years old and was in his twenty-ninth year as the Gay Head light keeper. He decided it was time to retire and sent a letter to Pleasonton requesting that his son, Ellis Skiff, replace him as keeper. By this time, Ellis Skiff had been helping his father with his duties and was familiar with the intricacies of caring for the lighthouse. Pleasonton forwarded Skiff's request to President John Quincy Adams:

> *Enclosed* [is the] *petition of Ebenezer Skiff, keeper of Gay Head Light, and Ellis Skiff, his son, praying that the latter may be appointed Keeper in the place of the former, who is disqualified by age; the appointment of Ellis Skiff is respectfully submitted.*
>
> *S.P. Pleasonton, Fifth Auditor.*

In 1828, Ellis Skiff assumed the position of principal keeper at the Gay Head Light. Keeper Ellis Skiff's beginning annual salary in 1828 was $350, which, at the time, was considered a relatively good annual income compared to other U.S. lighthouse keepers. Ellis Skiff served as the principal Gay Head Lighthouse keeper for seventeen years, from 1828 to 1845.

In 1834, at the age of eighty-three, Ebenezer Skiff died at home inside the extra room he had added onto the house. The photograph on the opposite page is of the 1816 Race Point Lighthouse located in Provincetown on Cape Cod. According to U.S. Coast Guard historians, the lantern room resting on top of this lighthouse is similar to the lantern room that sat on the 1799 Gay Head Light.

An 1816 photograph of the Race Point Light, whose lantern room was similar to Gay Head's 1799 lantern room. *Martha's Vineyard Museum.*

CHAPTER 6

BRICKS, MORTAR AND BROWNSTONE

Bricks, brownstone and special mortar—fitted to build Gay Head Light
mystery remains, from whence came the bricks, brownstone and labor

"WHERE DID THE BRICKS COME FROM?"

After producing several successful lighthouse fundraisers in the mid-1980s, VERI restored Gay Head Light to a condition suitable for public visitation. In the spring of 1987, we opened the door of the Gay Head Light to the public. This was the first time since 1957 that the light was available for public visits. Busloads of children from all the island's schools came to visit the lighthouse.

Over that first summer and fall in 1987, visitors to the light asked many questions. The most frequently asked question was: "Where did the bricks come from?"

Ferreting out answers to lighthouse questions had me meeting with members of the Wampanoag tribe of Gay Head; searching records at the Martha's Vineyard Museum; meeting with Elise Elliston, who lives next to the Chilmark brickyard, and librarian Hillary Wall at the *Martha's Vineyard Gazette*; and traveling to Nantucket, New Bedford, Providence and points around Boston. Like a large puzzle, the history of the Gay Head Light had pieces scattered across time. Each piece of the puzzle

A couple with three children visit the Gay Head Light, circa 1860. *Author's collection.*

offered clues to help find and fit other pieces—pieces that would help solve the palpable puzzle of the building of Martha's Vineyard's red brick lighthouse.

THE SO-CALLED CHILMARK BRICKYARD

According to Chilmark historian Peter Colt Josephs, who inherited a farm with a barn made of local brickyard bricks, "It is possible that small quantities of brick had been produced near the Roaring Brook site since the early 1700s." This attests to the antiquity of the brickyard located along Roaring Brook in Chilmark.

In 1836, a company named Smith and Barrows purchased a coastal property at the mouth of Roaring Brook in Chilmark. This property contained whatever brickyard was preexisting plus land containing a large deposit of clay. 1836 was also the year after the Great Fire of New York. This historic mid-winter fire in New York City was so huge that it raged across an estimated fifty acres and destroyed over six hundred buildings. High winds, freezing temperatures, an antiquated water delivery system and densely placed wooden buildings created a perfect firestorm scenario.

During reconstruction, the city required buildings to be constructed of stone and brick to help reduce fire hazards. This requirement generated a huge demand for the importation of bricks and stone. At about the same time, coastal and river cities like Boston, Providence, New Bedford, Newark and New Haven were experiencing a building boom. Increased demand for bricks was also fueled by America's Industrial Revolution, which required large quantities of high-quality firebricks as new ovens, furnaces and forges were developed.

To meet this demand, capitalists sought out, purchased and developed clay formations along the Northeast coast and its navigable rivers. Since there was no electricity, a natural source of energy was necessary for the success of any brickyard.

The energy used to run the Smith and Barrows brickyard in Chilmark was supplied by Roaring Brook. A series of stone-lined canals with manually adjusted wooden-plank flow dams guided and regulated the quantity and velocity of the gravity-fed water. These canals diverted the brook's water energy to turn a large water wheel. As the wheel turned, it provided the mechanical energy necessary to power the machines of the brick factory. While hydropower supplied the energy to run the machinery, the fuel to fire the kilns came from the island's woodlands.

BRICKS FOR THE GAY HEAD LIGHTHOUSE?

In the mid-1800s, the area surrounding the Chilmark brickyard developed into an early American industrial community. The community's economy was based on the mining of iron ore and clay, the manufacture of bricks, the making of paint products and the grinding grain into flour. These products were used on the island of Martha's Vineyard, as well as exported via schooner to points throughout the Northeast.

It is estimated that from the mid- to late 1800s, the bustling Chilmark brick factory was manufacturing up to 800,000 bricks a year. According to Preston Harris, whose ancestors once owned and operated the factory, his family met the demand by hiring up to seventy employees during the warmer months. During warmer months, French Canadian workers sailed down the coast to work at the brickyard. According to historian Peter Colt Josephs:

[To] help attract and keep workers through the busy season, the owners of the brick works provided on-site seasonal housing. Some of these houses were made with discarded bricks from the factory…The brick works was the largest business enterprise in the town of Chilmark, and one of the largest on the entire island.

When combined with the nearby paint mill, gristmill and iron ore mining operations, the area might have hosted up to one hundred seasonal workers. Housing and feeding such a large number of workers, some with families, resulted in the creation of a thriving but isolated coastal community. Drinking water for the community was readily available from Roaring Brook and Paint Mill Brook; fuel for heating homes was either shipped in or came from surrounding woodlands and peat bogs; corn flour was readily available from the nearby gristmill; neighboring farms provided a variety of foodstuffs; woodlands could be hunted; coastal fisheries could be fished; and there was always delivery of necessities by commercial ships.

This industrial community on Martha's Vineyard was one of the first to hire large numbers of seasonal workers during the summer months. In the Northeast, the demand for building bricks and firebricks was at its highest at this time, as the building industry was at its busiest.

Most of the construction of the brick Gay Head Lighthouse and keeper's house took place during the warm months between 1854 and 1856. Due to the thickness of the walls and the circumference and height of the lighthouse, the exacting work had to be accomplished with a crew of skilled masons and laborers. Besides hauling in brick to the site, tools, scaffolding equipment, constituents for mixing brick mortar, food and water also had to be transported to the site.

Shelter for the lighthouse construction crew might have been in the form of on-site camping, housing inside the barn and/or other outbuildings, a near-shore anchored boat with minimal amenities, or via an arrangement with neighboring Native Americans.

DELIVERING BRICKS BY SEA: MID-1800s

In the 1850s, there was a rough road from Chilmark to the town of Gay Head. Therefore, there is a possibility that the bricks used to build the lighthouse might have been transported overland from the brickyard.

In 1854, Smith and Barrows brick works had a deepwater dock. Schooners would secure themselves to the docks with lines to the dock and load up with bricks, clay, paint, iron ore and perhaps milled grain from the nearby gristmill. These goods were then transported throughout the Northeast. The schooners were designed to carry large loads of bricks. Certainly, it would have been easy for these ships to sail a few miles to the base of the Gay Head Cliffs. However, according to historic documents, until the year 1883, there was no dock facility for offloading bricks onto the beach near the lighthouse.

The Gay Head Light, which has walls that are five feet thick at its base, required a large quantity of clay bricks for its construction over two years. There was also a two-family brick keeper's house attached to the lighthouse.

There is no record of the federal government making financial provisions for construction of a dock during the construction of the first Gay Head Light in 1799 or during construction of the second lighthouse in the 1850s. There is, however, a record of travel between the lighthouse and the gristmill near the brickyard, as well as delivery of firewood by sea.

In 1803, Ebenezer Skiff, keeper of the Gay Head Light, influenced the selectmen of the town of Chilmark to send a letter on his behalf to the U.S. Lighthouse Establishment. The selectmen's letter expressed a list of hardships suffered by Skiff as a keeper, with the request to increase Skiff's annual $200 salary. The last sentence in this letter documents delivery of firewood by sea: "…his firewood must be brought by water and is not so easily obtained there as in seaport towns."

The letter also mentions that the Gay Head Light was nine miles from the nearest gristmill. As documented in this book, there was a gristmill in the early 1800s operating about nine miles from the lighthouse at the mouth of Roaring Brook, just above the brickyard.

The content of the selectmen's letter indicates that overland travel to the gristmill and its nearby brickworks was possible in 1803. On a similar note, transport by water of firewood to the lighthouse was also a functional reality, albeit on a limited basis.

According to all historic records, no dock existed near the clay cliffs until 1883. Therefore, the only delivery route for bricks from 1854 to 1856 was across the existing roads of Martha's Vineyard.

DELIVERING BRICKS AND MATERIALS
VIA VINEYARD ROADS: MID-1800s

The most plausible route in 1854 for transporting off-island materials to build the brick Gay Head Light was across the island via South Road from Edgartown Harbor.

The delivery of locally made bricks was also possible along a road from Chilmark brickyard to the lighthouse site. The method of hauling the loads of bricks would have probably been ox-drawn carts. Teams of oxen were common to many families and farms during this era.

Supporting this posture is a footnote on page thirty of Banks's 1911 *Annals of Gay Head* that is relative to the construction of the Gay Head brick light. From Banks, we learn about the cross-island transport of the heavy iron deck that makes up the floor of the watch room just below the lantern room. This iron deck sits on top of the uppermost brownstone and, according to records, was a challenge to transport and hoist into place because of its size and heavy weight. Again, if an unloading dock existed near the lighthouse during the construction of the Gay Head Light from 1854 to 1856, it would not have been necessary to have eight teams of oxen to "transport the iron deck across the island."

An ambiguous quote from Banks's book about constructing the Gay Head Light reads, "The work of construction at this remote point tested the capacity of the contractor. It required eight pair of oxen to transport the iron deck across the island and hoist it into position."

The lighthouse and its attached two-family keeper's house were made of bricks and would have required hundreds of wagonloads of bricks to construct.

Other information about the condition of roads between the Chilmark brickyard and the Gay Head Lighthouse can be found in *The History of Martha's Vineyard*, published in 1911. To quote Banks:

> One hundred years ago (c. 1811) a visitor to this town stated: "On the Indian lands there are no made roads, and for the most part only horse paths." This condition existed for about fifty years more, when a continuation of the county road from the Chilmark line to the lighthouse was laid out. Its construction was without design and unscientific, and soon became a continuous sand rut for lack of repairs. In 1870, when the town was incorporated, the act provided that the county commissioners

should forthwith "proceed to lay out and construct a road from Chilmark to the lighthouse on Gay Head, and may appropriate such sum from the funds of the county as may be necessary to defray the expense of the same." It was further provided that it should be maintained for five years by the state. This legislation resulted in the construction of the present and only public highway in the town, which since 1875 has been a town charge.

Giving testimony to traveling across Martha's Vineyard in 1838 is Samuel Adams Deven's book *Sketches of Martha's Vineyard*:

Although G. [Gay Head] is twenty miles from E. [Edgartown] and it is necessary in going thither to take down and put up, some thirty pairs of bars, it will well repay the perseverance of the visitor. A little more than an hour's ride from Gay Head, where you must alight from your chaise [carriage] and mount your horse...strike across the fields to the South Coast, overleaping a few walls and fences.

According to this 1838 book, there is no road that would have accepted a carriage or wagon within an hour's ride of Gay Head. This information is consistent with other reports from the era that mention how only horse and hiking trails existed in Gay Head.

A comparison of accessing Gay Head by sea or by land can be found in an 1841 publication by Edward Hitchcock, the "father of geology." In 1841, Hitchcock authored a seminal work entitled *Final Report on the Geology of Massachusetts*, published by J.H. Butler. While writing his book, Hitchcock visited Martha's Vineyard several times between 1823 and 1841 and was intrigued by the geology of the Gay Head Cliffs. In a footnote on page 275 of his book, Hitchcock shares his experiences of accessing Gay Head by sea and by land:

As it is extremely difficult to land a good-sized boat within several miles of Gay Head, the way, though the most expensive, of going thither upon the whole, is, to take passage at New Bedford in the steamboat, which launches at the other extremity of the Island, where a carriage can be procured to go to the Head. It is to be regretted, however, that the road for the last five or six miles is so rough and crooked, that a guide and considerable courage are indispensible. Not less than 17 pairs of bars must be gone through. At the Head, the traveler can be very comfortably lodged with an Indian by the name of Thomas Cooper. So far as I had intercourse with the aborigines residing here, I have been very favorably impressed with their shrewdness, industry, temperance, and general moral and religious character as a community.

The above paragraph provides significant information relative to there being no dock near the Gay Head Light in 1841, which made it difficult to access Gay Head via water. The above paragraph also tells us that the "brat way" or "spoiled person's way" was to travel to Gay Head via the road system. However, as expressed above, even road travel had its challenges.

DNA ANALYSES OF GAY HEAD LIGHT BRICKS

According to Dr. Denis Brosnan at Clemson University, bricks have a chemical analysis or assay reflecting their clay origin and mineral additions to the bricks. In molding of bricks, sand and natural stone fragments have been added to clay for centuries to reduce drying, shrinkage and cracking. Bricks are fired to an extent (or duration) to provide acceptable physical properties such as strength. Since bricks are porous, they will absorb water, and the measurement of water absorption is a characteristic of brick qualifying them for their ultimate placement in walls. Bricks with lower water absorption are used in outside walls since they are more resistant to freezing and thawing. The innermost bricks are used for structural purposes but do not necessarily need to be very low in water absorption since they are not normally exposed to water in the environment.

Dr. Brosnan and a team of scientists analyzed bricks from the interior of the Gay Head Light and from the kiln chimney at Chilmark brickyard. Even though the DNA of the bricks from the two sources was dissimilar, Dr. Brosnan said he could not come to a definitive conclusion at this time. According to Brosnan, depending on the specifications of the federal government, the clay used to make the bricks to build the lighthouse may very well have come from a different vein of clay than the clay used in the bricks to construct the chimney at the brickyard.

The author continues to work with Dr. Brosnan and others in an effort to determine the source of the lighthouse bricks for historicity.

ROARING BROOK'S GRISTMILL

Another important contribution to supporting the construction of the brick Gay Head Light would have been the gristmill located near the Chilmark brickyard. In Charles Gilbert Hine's 1908 book, *The Story of Martha's Vineyard*, he mentions that the gristmill was built in 1849 just above the brick works and that it was constructed by Francis Nye on the site of an earlier mill. Nye's gristmill could grind up to thirty bushels of corn a day. The same gristmill ground clay for making soap and paint. Based on this, we can surmise that the water-powered gristmill also supplied some of the food to sustain the workers who built the Gay Head Light from 1854 to 1856.

WHERE DID THE BROWNSTONE COME FROM?

Just as there is a dearth of information about the bricks to build the lighthouse, I also found local history repositories and newspapers to be void of information about the light's brownstone balcony.

My research of brownstone quarries operating during the three years that the brick Gay Head Light was under construction yielded only one viable source—the Portland Quarry in Connecticut. According to an 1880 census by researcher Alison C. Guiness, author of *Heart of Stone*, the Portland Quarry supplied up to 90 percent of the brownstone buildings and façades in New York City, Boston, New Haven and other cities. During its peak years of operation from 1850 to 1890, as many as 1,500 men were involved in the surveying, cutting and dressing of stone, while up to 150 yoke of oxen and sixty teams of horses were engaged in the lifting and transport of brownstone.

At the time of the construction of the brick Gay Head Light, the Portland Quarry was one of the few quarries (if not the only one) that had the ability to fulfill custom design orders from architects.

The shaping of brownstone to fulfill technical specifications requires special tools and knowledge. The five-tiered, cantilevered brownstone balcony on top of the Gay Head Light is a beautiful design. The brownstone is from the Mesozoic era of geologic time (200 million years ago). Besides its appeal to the eye, the brownstone serves as a balcony for viewers, a platform for maintenance and a system for supporting the lighting room.

The cantilevered brownstone balcony was imported from a quarry in Connecticut. *Author's collection.*

Most importantly, it provides a mass of weight to hold the structure to the ground during hurricanes.

On a related note, the Gay Head Light's brownstone was made during the time of the Great Famine in Ireland, also known as the Irish Potato Famine. During this time, many Irish people, including stonemasons, immigrated to America. Various sources mention that Irish stonemasons found employ with the Portland Quarry. Irish stonemasons were renowned for their abilities to build castles, churches and bridges.

Delivering brownstone from the Portland Quarry to Martha's Vineyard by sea would have been easily accomplished. The quarry's location near the Connecticut River allowed for convenient transport of brownstone to ports throughout the Northeast. During the quarry's peak years, it had up to forty custom-made schooners delivering brownstone to northeastern ports. Since the Cape Cod Canal (1914) had yet to be built, schooners carrying brownstone to Boston were frequently sailing past Martha's Vineyard.

However, similar to the mystery of transporting lighthouse bricks from Chilmark is the mystery as to which island port the brownstone was delivered. At the time, the only ports on the island were Holmes Hole and Edgartown. The road from Holmes Hole to Gay Head travels over a series of rock-strewn hills, valleys and streams. The southerly road from Edgartown to Gay Head was across relatively flat terrain until it reached Chilmark. Without doubt, the road from Edgartown to Gay Head would have been the easiest for teams of oxen to haul the heavy brownstone to the Gay Head Light.

There also lingers the remote possibility that the brownstone was offloaded at the Chilmark brickyard dock and transported overland.

DOCUMENTATION OF HAULING THE FRESNEL LENS

The early 1856 transport of the Fresnel lens and its supporting apparatus from the docks in Edgartown to the clay cliffs was reported in a reflective story published in the *Vineyard Gazette* on June 26, 1970:

> *It took eight yoke of oxen to transport the heavy iron railing for the catwalks...but it took 40 yoke of oxen to move the 60 frames of glass prisms and the multitudinous collection of machinery necessary to operate*

the new light. The finely balanced lantern weighed over a ton all told. It must have been a slow ponderous procession that traveled the 20 some odd miles of hard packed dirt and sandy island roads from the Edgartown wharf to the clay cliffs…

EPILOGUE

In closing, we may assume that the bricks used to build the Gay Head Light came from the Chilmark brickyard located at the mouth of Roaring Brook. During the three years the lighthouse was under construction (1854–56), the Smith and Barrows brick works, located nine miles distant in Chilmark, was producing hundreds of thousands of bricks each year. However, there remains a remote possibility that the U.S. Lighthouse Board contracted with off-island brick manufacturers for production and delivery of lighthouse bricks of certain specifications.

CHAPTER 7

DRINKING WATER CHALLENGES
AT GAY HEAD LIGHT

Remember well—the words from The Rime of the Ancient Mariner,
"Water, water, every where. Nor any drop to drink" when there is no well

SUED BY A LAWYER FOR A BROKEN LEG

In 1986, my nonprofit organization, VERI, received a thirty-five-year license from the U.S. Coast Guard to care for the Gay Head Light. Within the first year, VERI was sued for $140,000.

VERI was sued by a female lawyer from Illinois as a result of injuries she sustained while standing near the Gay Head Light. Like many tourists, this woman walked toward the lighthouse from the parking area near the shops. The woman proceeded to walk up the hill so she could have a better perspective for taking her pictures. As she stood taking photographs, the earth beneath her collapsed, and she fell into a circular hole that was covered by rotting boards. The fall resulted in the woman suffering a broken leg with a compound fracture. The language in her lawsuit claimed that the Gay Head Light was an "attractive nuisance" that presented a danger to the public. Upon close inspection, it was discovered that the hole she fell into was once an old cistern used for storing water. Of course, the lawsuit contained language such as, "pain and suffering," "disfigurement" and "loss of income."

As president of VERI, I requested the plot plan of record from the U.S. Coast Guard. The USCG sent me a 1924 plot plan that had been updated in 1960. Using the 1960 plot plan, we did a new survey. Fortunately, the cistern the woman fell into was ten feet outside the lighthouse property line.

1799: STORING RAIN WATER AND CARTING SPRING WATER

Finding and storing good drinking water and capturing and storing good rainwater in the clay cliff area of Gay Head was always a challenge for lighthouse keepers. Throughout the history of the Gay Head Lighthouse, keepers and their families faced a variety of challenges in obtaining safe drinking water.

As will be explained Chapter 13 of this book, contaminated water at Gay Head Lighthouse was suspected in the illnesses of several adults and the tragic deaths of a handful of children. From 1799 to 1956, every Gay Head Lighthouse keeper explored a variety of methods to secure safe drinking water for his family.

The first record relative to drinking water at the Gay Head Lighthouse occurred on June 7, 1799. On that date, the *New Bedford Marine Journal* published the specifications for the Vineyard's first lighthouse. These specifications were published for the purpose of soliciting bids. The bidding specifications were broken down under several headings, including sections for a water storage cistern and a well:

> *The Cistern must be made perfectly tight, and then set in the best clay mortar, eight inches deep under the bottom, and like good mortar on the sides, so as to fill up the vacancy between the Cistern and the wall; great attention must paid to the goodness of the mortar, it must be free from lumps, and be better, if possible, than the best made for laying bricks. The Cisterns are to be covered with pine planks. The entrance into the Vault must be secured by a good door, hung on iron hinges, and a good lock.*
>
> *A Well is to be sunk as near the House as may be, where one may be had by digging from twenty to thirty feet, and to be well stoned up, and to be provided with a bucket and the machinery for drawing water—provided the Spring in the edge of the Cliff shall not supply water sufficient for a family.*

The above 1799 bid specifications were probably composed by personnel serving in the newly formed United States Lighthouse Establishment. These specifications appear to be standard bid details used in the building of any lighthouse or house in the Northeast. Apparently, the off-island bureaucrats had little understanding about the glacial clay formation of Gay Head, which had always presented challenges when it came to finding an adequate supply of safe drinking water.

After taking the job as "Keeper of the Gayhead Light," Ebenezer Skiff moved his family onto the lighthouse grounds in November 1799. On November 18, 1799, he ignited the whale oil lamp that cast the first-ever beam of light out to sea from Gay Head. Thus, Skiff's daily chore of keeping the light burning every night from dusk to dawn was initiated. As can be imagined, there had to be considerable labor in setting up materials to run the lighthouse. This was in addition to the materials necessary for family survival, which included home furnishings, food, good drinking water and firewood.

When Skiff accepted employment as lighthouse keeper, he had no idea as to what his salary would be. For the first few months, he worked without pay as he waited to learn the amount of his annual salary.

FINDING FIREWOOD

With winter coming on, Skiff found that there was little firewood in the local area. To make things more difficult, the roads to wooded areas were nearly nonexistent. So Skiff had to rely on shallow-draft boats bringing firewood from other areas of the island. As he spent money in preparation of winter, Skiff wondered if the cost of firewood was going to be paid for by the U.S. Lighthouse Establishment. Running low on money, Skiff sent a letter of inquiry about what his salary was going to be, along with a bill for the firewood he purchased for $25.93.

The New Bedford lighthouse superintendent, Edward Pope, forwarded Skiff's letter to Washington, and upon receipt of reply, Skiff received the following message on March 4, 1800:

> *The President of the United States has been pleased to fix the Salary of the Keeper of the Light House at Gayhead at 200 Dollars per annum...The Keeper's charge for Wood introduced in your Account will not be admitted, as nothing of the kind is allowed to Persons employed in similar situations.*

Certainly, Skiff's situation was not "similar" to that of other lighthouse keepers in the region. At the time, few, if any, lighthouses were located in such a desolate area without trees or drinking water.

In 1803, after three years on the job, Ebenezer Skiff was still being paid only $200 a year. Finding himself overworked and underpaid, Skiff had much to complain about.

In August 1803, Skiff sent another letter to Edward Pope in New Bedford. It was Pope who supervised the bidding process for the construction of the Gay Head Light and who acted as liaison between Skiff and the U.S. Lighthouse Establishment. As published in February 1982, by Arthur Railton in the *Dukes County Intelligencer*, Ebenezer Skiff thought he deserved more than $200 a year, as well as a better supply of drinking water for his family. Skiff's letter of complaint to Pope read, in part:

> *The land is very poor and is only two acres…but so much of it as I have manured fully, answered the purposes you expected. I cannot do without the use of a horse, which I am obliged to keep in a common [Wampanoag] pasture which is a considerable distance from me. My firewood is costly… the spring water does not affect a sufficiency in the summer. I depend chiefly upon my salary for the support of my family. I have enclosed…a certificate from the Selectmen stating my situation.*

The "selectmen" Keeper Skiff refers to were those from the town of Chilmark. Chilmark was the nearest white settlement and the town where Skiff and his family resided prior to moving onto the lighthouse property.

Mustering a show of support for Skiff, the three Chilmark selectmen— Mathew Mayhew Jr., Ephraim Mayhew and Stephen Tilton—wrote a letter to Edward Pope. Amongst other things, the subject of ongoing water problems at the Gay Head Lighthouse is again emphasized in the selectmen's letter:

> *We, the subscribers, Selectmen of Chilmark, hereby certify that Ebenezer Skiff, keeper of the light house on Gayhead in said Town, dwells about four miles from the nearest white people, six miles from a district school, nine miles from the meetinghouse and nearly the same distance from a gristmill—the way is hilly and bad in the common way of passing and there are creeks which are scarcely fordable at all seasons. The spring in the Clift [sic] where he dwells yields poor water at best and will not afford a sufficiency for a family. In dry seasons he has to cart water from a brook*

nearly one mile distant—his firewood must be brought by water and is not so easily obtained there as in seaport towns…His situation is uncommonly boisterous and the pasturage which he is obliged to hire of the natives is generally very inconvenient. Said Skiff we esteem a reputable man faithful to the publick [sic] and deserving of encouragement.

After waiting two years, Skiff received no reply to his letter—nor did the Chilmark selectmen receive a reply to their request on Skiff's behalf for financial relief.

On October 25, 1805, Skiff sent another letter. This letter again complained about water problems at the Gay Head Lighthouse. The following copy of Skiff's letter is from the National Archives:

Sir: Clay and Oker [sic] of different colours from which this place derived its name ascend in a sheet of wind from the high Clifts [sic] and catch on the light House Glass, which often requires cleaning on the outside—tedious service in cold weather, and additional to what is necessary in any other part of the Massachusetts. The spring of water in the edge of the Clift [sic] is not sufficient. I have carted almost the whole of the water used in my family during the last Summer and until this Month commenced, from nearly one mile distant. These impediments were neither known nor under Consideration at the time of fixing my Salary. I humbly pray you to think of me, and (if it shall be consistent with your wisdom) increase my Salary. And in duty bound I am yours to Command. EBENEZER SKIFF, Keeper of Gayhead [sic] Light House

Due to his persistence—and perhaps the evolving persuasiveness of his pen—Skiff's letter was successful in swaying the lighthouse governing body into granting him a fifty-dollar-per-year increase in salary.

All was well until about 1812, when the lighting machinery was changed at the Gay Head Light. With a rotating light, Skiff found himself and his family overwhelmed with extra work. Staying true to character, Skiff wrote another letter of complaint requesting a pay increase. In answer to Skiff's letter, President Madison authorized another fifty-dollar-per-year increase in Skiff's salary.

In 1820, Ebenezer Skiff was still laboring as keeper of the Gay Head Light. Getting on in years, the task of obtaining water for his family from a mile-distant spring was becoming a major burden. Skiff wrote another letter of complaint, this time addressed to Stephen Pleasonton, fifth auditor of the treasury.

Pleasonton had recently been appointed by President Monroe as the new administrator of lighthouses. In his letter to Pleasonton, Skiff asked for a cart and casks to use in the fetching of water, inasmuch as the spring on which he had relied had given out. Pleasonton asked how much it would cost and then authorized the local lighthouse superintendent "to procure a pair of wheels and water casks for the use of the Keeper of Gayhead Light House, provided the expense shall not exceed the sum you state, viz., fifty dollars."

In January 1828, Ebenezer Skiff, who was now in his mid-seventies, wrote a letter to Pleasonton requesting that his son, Ellis, take over the job of keeper of the light at Gay Head. Skiff's letter was forwarded to President John Quincy Adams with a cover letter from Pleasonton that read, "Enclosed petition of Ebenezer Skiff, keeper of Gay Head Light, and Ellis Skiff, his son, praying that the latter may be appointed Keeper in the place of the former, who is disqualified of age; the appointment of Ellis Skiff is respectfully submitted."

President Adams approved Ellis Skiff as the new keeper.

From 1799 to 1839, the father-and-son Skiff team had weathered many challenges and seen many changes at the Gay Head Light. But after almost forty years of living at the Gay Head Light, the Skiff family continued to face challenges in securing a safe and reliable source of drinking water.

In 1839, the cistern that stored rainwater for the Skiff family was leaking. A leaking cistern not only loses water into surrounding soil but also, at times of heavy rain, can experience water infiltration into the system. Such surface water infiltration into a cistern can contaminate the water, which in this case was probably used for bathing and washing household items such as eating utensils. There was also the need for sufficient water for the all-important job of cleaning the glass in the lighthouse light room and other fixtures to keep the light shining bright.

Skiff requested a new cistern from his new on-island lighthouse supervisor, John P. Norton of Edgartown. Fulfilling Skiff's request, Norton secured finances for a new stone cistern to be installed by a local contractor. However, the cistern's stonework was not installed properly, and the cistern was prone to leakage. This leakage allowed the red clay fines to infiltrate the cistern's water.

Clay fines are naturally colloidal and therefore easily become suspended in water. At the Gay Head Cliffs, it is also this property that allows clay to become suspended in ocean water and visible to the eye as it creates a colorful plume floating out to sea.

Norton sent a letter explaining the problem to Edward Pleasonton in March 1840: "The cistern water is not fit for culinary purposes, owing to the red Ochre blowing on the roof of the house which causes the water to be red and thick, although very useful for other purposes."

Obtaining good drinking water never ceased as a topic of concern and conversation at Gay Head Light. Besides dealing with the leaking cistern problem in 1840, Skiff also faced a new challenge in his effort to secure safe drinking water for his family. In another letter to John Norton, Skiff wrote:

> *I think it necessary that the Government provide a Road from this establishment to the spring where my predecessor* [Skiff's father, Ebenezer] *and myself have obtained our supply of water for about thirty years for the following reasons:*

> *The distance is about half a mile across fields belonging to the Indians and people of Colour, one of which has fenced in the spring and has commenced ploughing the land all around the spring…another has dug a cellar and is about building a dwelling house in the road that I have cleared out and used for several years…The spring was fitted with a stone reservoir so that the water is led into the cask while they are on the truck. The reservoir was made by my predecessor and a Coloured man who is dead…I have no doubt but the Indians are still willing that I should obtain my water as usual if it could be done without injuring them. I feel quite reluctant in making any more requests respecting water, but under the existing circumstances I deem it my duty. Please make this communication known to the Hon. Stephen Pleasonton, Esq.*

Ellis Skiff's 1840 letter was forwarded to Pleasonton. Norton suggested to Pleasonton that since the deeded rights to access the water were unclear, it might be best to pay the Indians a "reasonable price, say $40." Since there is no other correspondence on this subject, this matter was apparently resolved by Skiff purchasing a right of access to the spring water from the Indians.

From 1840 to the early 1920s, there is little mention of water problems at the lighthouse. We can only assume that the access and water rights to the nearby spring that Skiff purchased were adequate to serve the needs of keepers that followed.

AN OFFICIAL WATER REPORT IN 1922

On March 13, 1922, the superintendent of the First Lighthouse District answered the following questions on the federal "Form 60" about the drinking water quality at the Gay Head Lighthouse:

- *How procured? Rain water from dwelling roof*
- *Quality? Good*
- *Quantity ample or not for the station at all seasons of the year? Ample*
- *Liable or not to be injured by the inroads of storm tides and seas? No*
- *If rain water in tanks or cisterns, what precautions have been taken to insure purity? Frequent cleaning*
- *Capacity of tanks or cisterns, and where placed?*
  1 in Keeper's cellar—900 gallons
  1 in Ass't Keeper's cellar—900 gallons
  1 on east side of dwelling—3,800 gallons
- *Tanks or cisterns of what materials made? Bricks—cement plastered*
- *Is there a distilling apparatus at the station? None*
- *If from a well, describe and give depth. None*
- *Are there any local causes, such as swamps, marshes, etc., in the immediate vicinity of the lighthouse which are likely to be causes of disease? No*
- *Would draining or other artificial means employed on the lighthouse premises be likely to improve the sanitary condition of the light station? No*

The above question-and-answer form gives the impression that the rainwater captured in the cisterns is of adequate quality for use as drinking water. Such information on this form was completely false. It is as though the bureaucrat who filled out this form wanted to protect himself and his superiors by submitting false information.

It is curious that there is no mention of Gay Head Light keeper Charles W. Vanderhoop Sr. obtaining his family's drinking water from a spring that was about one mile distant.

The water problem at the keeper's house reared its head again during the tour of Keeper Frank A. Grieder. After World War II, Grieder's wife, Elsie, picked up her pen and wrote letters of complaint about the water situation. As in 1799, the keeper's house was still collecting rainwater for bathing, washing dishes and clothing (by hand), watering the garden and cleaning the lighthouse prisms, glass and brass. As in 1799, outhouses continued to serve as toilets, and commodes were used when weather or timing made a trip to the outhouse impractical.

As with Ebenezer Skiff, the first Gay Head Light keeper, Elise Grieder's letter of complaint was mailed to the president of the United States. In Elise Grieder's 1946 letter, she complained to President Harry S. Truman about the lack of water for her family and how disappointed she was with our powerful government. Within her letter of complaint was a request for a flush toilet, a bathtub and indoor plumbing for running water. In 1946, when Elsie Grieder wrote her letter, a certain number of houses in Gay Head already had flush toilets and indoor plumbing.

Within three weeks after mailing her letter, Elise Grieder received a reply from staff at the White House. The U.S. Coast Guard was making plans to electrify the new lookout tower being planned for construction near the brick lighthouse. Once electricity was available on the lighthouse property, Elise Grieder would have all her wishes fulfilled.

The Grieder family left the Gay Head Light property in 1948.

Following in Keeper Grieder's footsteps was Keeper Joseph Hindley. The Hindleys lived at the lighthouse from 1948 to 1956 and were the last family to serve as keepers of the Gay Head Light. Due to Elsie Grieder's letters, the Hindleys briefly enjoyed a house that was electrified in 1953. Once electrified, the house was improved with indoor plumbing that provided running water to bathrooms and the kitchen.

In 1982, Keeper Hindley's surviving daughter, Betty Hatzikon of Falmouth, Massachusetts, wrote a letter to the Dukes County Historical Society. The contents of her letter reflected on being raised at the Gay Head Light from 1950 to 1956. As with every keeper family who ever lived at the Gay Head Light, water again was a major topic of note in Betty Hatzikon's letter.

Even though this letter will be expressed in its entirely in another section of this book, the paragraph about drinking water is presented here:

> *Before we were transferred* [in 1956], *the house had been completely modernized with all conveniences, including running water—which you couldn't drink. Until the day we left we had to get our drinking water from one of the two freshwater springs in Gay Head.*

CHAPTER 8

GAY HEAD LIGHT PAINTED WITH RED CLAY!

*The lady painted herself red—to catch sea-weary eyes of passing sailors
they told stories of times when lost at sea—dreams of the lady in red*

Over the past thirty years, I have viewed many photographs of the Gay Head Light and its keeper's house. I noticed in some vintage photographs that the brick exterior of the lighthouse appeared as one color. At first, I assumed the photographs were hand-painted or that the color was manipulated in the dark room. However, there was also the incongruity of all the bricks being the same color.

We know the bricks used to build the Gay Head Light came from multicolored fired clay of various densities and that the bricks were manufactured by an antiquated kiln process. As a result, the handmade bricks were of many colors due to inconsistent drying and firing temperatures.

On a similar note, various vintage photographs depict the white mortar joints between the bricks of the lighthouse as the same color as the bricks. In fact, in a few old photographs, the white mortar joints of the bricks appear as though they, too, are made from red clay.

Originally, I passed off these incongruities as being a failure of the photograph to accurately depict the image of the brick exterior of Gay Head Light.

In 1985, while researching the history of the Gay Head Light in preparation for congressional testimony about Martha's Vineyard lighthouses and lighthouses in general, I came across a document entitled "Gay Head

Light-Station, Mass. MEMORANDA OF CESSIONS, by Massachusetts."
This document contained a series of timeline notes about the lighthouses of
Massachusetts. Relative to Gay Head Light, item number 97 from the year
1874 reads:

> *Gay Head, on southwest point of Martha's Vineyard, Mass.—The
> exterior of the light-tower has been repainted and the barn new silled,
> shingled, and whitewashed. On the 15th of May, 1874, the light at this
> station was changed from flashing-white by making every fourth flash red.*

This document provided me with an exact date that the light's
signal was converted to include red flashes. It also provided the first
documentation confirming my assumption that from about 1856 to the
early 1900s, the Gay Head Light's exterior was probably painted. The
use of the words "the exterior of the light-tower has been repainted"
is a clear indication that the exterior of the Gay Head Light was being
painted on a recurring basis.

Helping to research the lighthouse bricks is a Dr. Denis A. Brosnan,
bishop chair at Clemson University's Department of Materials and Science
Engineering. Dr. Brosnan has been the lead scientist in analyzing the bricks
used to build the Gay Head Light. When he first approached the Gay Head
Light project, Dr. Brosnan assumed that the exterior of the Gay Head Light,
like most brick lighthouses, had been whitewashed on its exterior to help it
survive the corrosive salt air and sea spray. The sealing of the exterior of
the brick with whitewash helps prevent deterioration and crumbling of the
mortar joints and corrosion of the iron components that help hold brick
lighthouses together.

Research during this book project revealed that the exterior bricks of the
Gay Head Light were sealed with a protective layer of paint in past years.
Research also revealed that the interior bricks were sealed with a protective
layer of whitewashed plaster. The sealing of the exterior and interior of the
lighthouse bricks would have contributed to the longevity of the structure
we see today.

The following documentation from the Gay Head Light keeper's logs of
1898–99 provide further support of the exterior of the light being painted:

> *May 12, 1898: Commenced Painting tower*
> *May 8, 1899: Commenced Painting in the tower*
> *May 13, 1899: Finished painting in the tower*

May 15, 1899: Painted outside of the lantern
May 17, 1899: Commenced Painting the tower
July 16, 1899: Painting the Tower
July 17, 1899: Painting the Tower

The fact that the Gay Head Light keeper recorded that he "Finished Painting in the tower" and then two days later wrote "Commenced Painting the tower" is an indication that the keepers were painting both the inside and outside of the tower.

In February 2014, I found an official U.S. Lighthouse Service document dated March 13, 1922. This document indicates that the Gay Head Light was painted with red paint. The body of this report describes in detail the parts that make up the whole of the Gay Head Light. The report contains 144 enumerated line items, each item with a blank space to be filled out by the inspecting officer of the U.S. Lighthouse Service.

The inspecting officer of this 1922 report was T.J. Morse, first assistant superintendent of the U.S. Lighthouse Service. Presented below are relevant portions of the inspector's report (I highlighted #18):

STATION

1. *By whom described: T.J. Morse, 1ˢᵗ Asst. Supt., Date: March 13, 1922*
2. *Name of Station: Gay Head*
3. *Characteristic of light: Group flash white; alternate red flash every 40 seconds, 3 white and 1 red flashes (Eclipse 5 seconds flash 5 seconds duration)*
4. *Geographical position of light: Latitude, 41° 20' 55"; Longitude, 70° 50' 08"*
5. *Location: On west point of Martha's Vineyard Island*

PREMISES

6. *Origin of title to site of station: Ceded by the Commonwealth of Massachusetts*
7. *Date of reservation, deed, lease, or permission to occupy: Act, February 22, 1799*
8. *Area of entire site: about 2 acres; (b) area enclosed: Entire; (c) type of fence: Wooden fence and stone wall*

9. Distance of tower from nearest high-water mark: About 500 feet

10. Wharf or land on premises: None

11. Means by which the light station may be reached and distance to nearest post office or town, with name: Public road from Vineyard Haven, 20 miles; Gay Head Post Office, Mass, 1 mile

12. Tower or other means for supporting the lantern and apparatus: Tower

13. Number of separate lights: One

14. When first built or established: 1799

15. When last thoroughly rebuilt, repaired, renovated: 1856

16. Height of focal plane of lantern above mean high water (on sea and gulf coasts): 170 feet

17. Background of the lighthouse, upon which it is projected, as seen from seaward: Sky

18. Color of tower, and how produced: Red—paint

Number 18 on this list indicates that the color of the Gay Head tower was produced by red paint. As expressed earlier, this was not the first time I had read about the Gay Head Light being painted red. In addition to this discovery, I also found documentation indicating that the red paint used on the Gay Head Light was probably made from our island's red clay.

At first, I assumed that documents were incorrectly referring to the red color of the bricks. However, when reviewing certain vintage photographs, it became obvious that all the bricks on the exterior of the light were of the same red color, as were the joints of the bricks and, in some photos, the stones of the brownstone balcony and its mortar joints. Apparently, the entire light, from top to bottom, may have been painted red at one time. Other vintage photographs show all the bricks as being painted but not the brownstone. Also, depending on the photograph or postcard printer, similar vintage illustrations sometimes vary in color tone. Regardless, the brick appears to be coated with paint. The best documentation I have discovered regarding the Gay Head Light being painted with red clay was in an 1892 handwritten manuscript from M.B. Safford of the U.S. Coast and Geodetic Survey. A section of Safford's letter reads, "Gay Head Light is painted with red clay mixed with oil."

The appearance of a red-painted lighthouse in photographs is consistent with documentation of red paint being applied to the exterior. It should be noted for the record that some lighthouse postcard photographs were hand-painted and may or may not accurately depict the light's true color.

A man named Bill Grieder used to live at the Gay Head Light Station when his father, Frank, was keeper, from 1937 to 1948. In an interview in 2000 for *Lighthouse Digest*, Grieder recalled painting and whitewashing the lighthouse:

> *There was always some work for me. I used to polish brass. I learned to light the lighthouse, and I taught my mother to do it. There were times when my Dad was sick—my Mum would go up to light the light or I would go up. Of course we had an assistant keeper, but if you couldn't call on him, you did it yourself.*
>
> *I went up to help whitewash or paint the tower, and mow the lawn of course. Lug the kerosene up in the tower. Polish the lens. It had to be cleaned and dusted all the time. We had a dust cover over that.*

According to official U.S. Lighthouse Service documents, the outside of the Gay Head Light was painted red. The inside walls of the tower were plastered and periodically whitewashed. Plaster walls have to be whitewashed to keep them sealed and to fill in any cracks that might occur. This information explains and corroborates Bill Grieder's statement about helping to "whitewash and paint the tower."

If a vintage photograph of the painted lighthouse is in black and white, the entire exterior appears as one dark color. On the other hand, if the lighthouse goes for years without the bricks being painted, the paint deteriorates and is removed by weather, exposing the multicolored bricks and white mortar joints.

In modern photographs of the brick lighthouse, the fact that it's unpainted becomes obvious. The bricks on the exterior of the lighthouse come in a variety of light and dark colors. This is mostly a result of the uneven firing of the bricks in the kilns. Variations of heat combined with the bricks' locations during the firing process create different-colored bricks. The temperature at which a brick is fired determines its color. The dark reds, dark browns and black-colored bricks are usually the result of exposure to higher temperatures.

MAKING RED PAINT ON MARTHA'S VINEYARD

The wonder of doing historical research is finding forgotten facets of our island's past. Once I found reputable documentation that our Gay Head Light was painted red, I remembered reading about the manufacture of red paint from the island's red clay.

"Is it possible," I asked myself, "that the Gay Head Light was painted with locally made red paint?"

Subsequently, I learned that making paint from dry clay was a simple process often used on Martha's Vineyard. Chunks of the desired color of clay were removed from the cliffs, broken into small pieces and allowed to dry in the sun. Once the clay was dry, it was brought to a mill for grinding into a fine powder that was then placed into wooden barrels for transport and/or sale.

If a paint project was relatively small, the dry clay could be pulverized by hand into powder with a heavy instrument. This fine powder was known as "paint" in the late 1800s. When it came time to undertake a painting project, the powdered clay was simply blended with linseed oil to create a liquid similar to the paint we use today. The thickness of the clay paint was determined by how much oil was used. Just as today, different thicknesses of paint are used for different purposes.

When I reviewed various vintage photographs of the "painted" Gay Head Light, I noticed that the paint was applied so thickly that it was difficult to discern the mortar joints of the bricks. The same red clay paint used to paint the lighthouse was also used to paint the keeper's house. For this reason, many photographs depict the lighthouse and the keeper's house as having the same red color.

PAINT MANUFACTURING AT ROARING BROOK AND PAINT MILL BROOK

Paint was made at a gristmill located about a half mile upstream from the mouth of Roaring Brook brickyard. This paint mill along Roaring Brook was known as the Mt. Prospect Paint Mill and was operated by various owners from about 1847 to about 1862. From all indications, it appears as though the Mt. Prospect Paint Mill was capable of producing enough paint in the mid-1800s to be a viable source of paint for the Gay Head Light. According to Charles Banks, the highest annual production of this clay paint mill was about forty-six thousand pounds of dried paint pigment.

A short distance to the east of Roaring Brook is Paint Mill Brook. According the *Vineyard Gazette*, a paint mill known as the Carpet Mill Factory was established at the mouth of this brook in about 1865. The name of this factory was derived from the major end-use of the clay paint in the production of naturally dyed carpets.

According to census records, the Carpet Mill Factory paint mill produced 750 tons of "ochre" clay paint from June 1, 1869, to June 1, 1870. Most of this paint was shipped to major New England markets. This clay paint factory produced mostly red and yellow clay paints, which means that it could have easily supplied red paint for the Gay Head Light.

CHAPTER 9

LIGHTHOUSE KEEPERS
AND THE SECRET MILITARY

Those who prepare for battle—must make war or serve no purpose
from Maine to Galveston keepers watched for ships—no loose lips

GAY HEAD LIGHT WIRED DIRECTLY TO WASHINGTON

Prior to 1898, the Gay Head Light and the nearby U.S. Life-Saving Service were wired with telegraph and telephone lines by the U.S. military division known as the Signal Service. In a report dated June 30, 1887, and entitled "Annual Report of the Chief Signal Officer to the Secretary of War," page 140 reads:

> *On Martha's Vineyard, Massachusetts, a telephone line, 15 miles in length, was built from Cedar Tree Neck to Gay Head Light-House, to permit the display of cautionary signals at that point, as well as for use in case of wrecks. Lieut. J.H. Weber, Signal Corps, assumed charge of the lines on Martha's Vineyard and Nantucket on August 18, 1886.*
>
> *The following sections of sea-coast lines remain in operation July 1, 1887, viz:*
>
> *Norfolk to Hatteras, including Cape Charles Branch............194 miles*
> *Wilmington to Southport.....................................30 miles*
> *Block Island to Narragansett Pier..............................31 miles*
> *Wood's Holl to Nantucket, including Gay Head Branch...........76 miles*

On September 25, 1890, the Gay Head Light keeper wrote the following: "Telephone installed [for use by] Signal Service."

Throughout my thirty-four years of involvement with the Gay Head Light, I was never aware of the dual purpose of the lighthouse serving as an aid to navigation and as a Spanish-American War outpost connected directly to the Office of Naval Intelligence in Washington.

As quoted in the above report, the chief signal officer reported to the secretary of war. The public's perception of the Signal Service was that it was for the purpose of reporting weather—not military secrets.

WATCHING FOR THE ENEMY IN THE SPANISH-AMERICAN WAR

When war broke out with Spain, the U.S. Navy Department, with the assistance of its War College, had already designed a national signal system for use by coastal patrols. Each coastal state had naval militia drilled in the various methods of communicating with ships with flags. With telegraph and telephone lines already in place, communication with the Office of Naval Intelligence in Washington was now possible between coastal outposts, lighthouses and offshore ships.

On May 1, 1898, just one week after Spain declared war on America, a letter was published from Block Island stating that residents were in fear of bombardment. Shortly afterward, newspapers reported that Block Island had been totally destroyed by a Spanish cruiser. War headlines raged in papers across America. On May 13, the headlines of a New England paper reported, "Coming here! Spanish war-ships reported off the Grand Banks!"

MILITARIZATION OF LIGHT KEEPERS AND LIGHTHOUSES

Once war broke out in April 1898, 850 lighthouse keepers manning 243 lighthouses from Maine to Galveston, Texas, were required to report suspicious shipping traffic to the War Board in Washington.

The enlisted men of the U.S. Coast Signal Service were divided into watches; the lighthouse keepers were on duty twenty-four hours every day, and the lifesaving stations not only "watched" the coast but also patrolled beaches between stations.

Gay Head Light keepers were constantly scanning and reporting passing ships. At the same time, Gay Head's U.S. Life-Saving personnel were patrolling the Gay Head beach. This rigorous regimen of lighthouse keepers being on high alert at the Gay Head Light began in April 1898 and concluded at the end of the war four months later.

Reports of suspicious ships were wired to Washington daily. Communication of shipping information or with "outsiders" (civilians and media) was forbidden, and secrecy was enforced.

GUNS AT GAY HEAD LIGHT

According to a 1901 article authored by Captain John Russell Bartlett and entitled "Watching for the Enemy in the Spanish War" (*Century Illustrated Magazine*), each field outpost, including Gay Head Light, was supplied with Springfield rifles, international code flags and related code books, wigwag flags (with cones and drums for calm weather), powerful binoculars, spyglasses and telescopes.

During the Spanish-American War, the U.S. Navy and Merchant Marines were apprised of U.S. Coast Signal Service locations so they could transmit and receive military information about the enemy. There were thirty-six strategic signal locations established along America's coast. The stations considered the most significant by the military were "Baker's Island near Bar Harbor, Cape Elizabeth, Isle of Shoals, Cape Ann, Cape Cod, Gay Head, Block Island, Montauk Point, Cape Henry, etc., and so on to Galveston."

Every ship that passed along any section of America's coast, including Gay Head, was immediately reported to the U.S. Navy Department in Washington.

THE END OF THE SPANISH-AMERICAN WAR

When Commodore Dewey was ordered to engage the Spanish fleet in the East, the U.S. Navy Department knew the approximate location of all enemy vessels. Photographs of the Spanish ships were reproduced in book form and circulated to all lighthouse keepers, lifesaving personnel and enlisted Signal Service members. These photographs helped coastal watchers identify enemy warships and their fuel supply vessels. Besides photographs of each type of enemy ship, there was also information on the size of the crew and the firepower of each particular enemy ship.

Shortly after the war ended, the U.S. Coast Signal Service was shut down. The enlisted Signal Service men were discharged from the naval service, and the gear and all portable property was stored away in the closest navy yard. At the same time, all light keepers and lifesaving personnel were relieved of their quasi-military status and required communication with the Office of Naval Intelligence.

All war-related telegraph and telephone wires installed at lighthouses, such as those at Gay Head Light, were turned over to the U.S. Lighthouse Service.

WORLD WAR II BUNKERS (PILLBOXES)

The World War II scenario played out in similar fashion at the Gay Head Light area.

In 1939, the U.S. Coast Guard military branch took control of the U.S. Bureau of Lighthouses. This was the first time in U.S. history that a U.S. military branch had taken over a civilian branch. By World War II, all U.S. lighthouses and other aids to navigation were under control of the U.S. military.

Similar to the Spanish-American War, both the Gay Head Light and Coast Guard Station Gay Head were under strict military orders to be on vigilant lookout for the enemy—especially submarines. Two concrete bunkers were set up on top of the clay cliffs and were staffed by full-time military personnel. The correct term for the concrete structures set up near the lighthouse is "pillboxes." However, over the years, these two concrete structures became known colloquially as "bunkers."

According to Ann Vanderhoop, who, with her husband, Luther Madison, owned the restaurant at the head of the cliffs during the war, "The entire circle and head of the cliff was blocked off with barricades. The troops assigned to the bunkers were heavily armed and had what appeared to be large mounted cannons on top of the bunkers and rifles and machine guns inside the bunkers." In other words, the U.S. military was prepared to repel · any enemy invasion along the Gay Head coastal region.

One of the two bunkers was situated north of the lighthouse, near where Coast Guard Station Gay Head tower used to be. I took a photograph of the northern bunker in 1972, when it was near the top of the cliffs. Today, it rests in the tidal zone below the cliffs. The second bunker to the south was set up where the tourist lookout is now located. The top of the square concrete bunker is still visible in the center of the lookout area. The roof of the buried bunker is topped off with a stone set in concrete and embellished with an inscribed bronze plaque.

For information about World War II on Martha's Vineyard, see Thomas Dresser's book *World War II on Martha's Vineyard*.

CHAPTER 10

BILL GRIEDER'S BOYHOOD AT GAY HEAD LIGHT: 1937-48

*A child's memories of lighthouse duties—are easy to romanticize
we the readers are easily seduced as we imagine and fantasize*

Back in the 1920s, Bill Grieder's father, Frank A. Grieder, lived in Camden, Maine, with his wife, Elsie, and their two sons. Elsie was originally from England, where she served as a sergeant cook in the Royal Air Force during World War I. Frank worked in a granite quarry. In 1930, at the height of the Depression, everything changed for the Grieder family when Frank took a job with the U.S. Lighthouse Service. Frank Grieder's son Bill was in first grade when his father became the light keeper at Duxbury Pier Light in Massachusetts.

The Grieder family packed their belongings into a Model A and left Maine for the town of Rocky Nook in Massachusetts. Rocky Nook was located near Duxbury Pier Light (Bug Light), where Frank Grieder served as keeper from 1930 to 1934. In 1934, Frank Grieder was transferred to Great Point Light on Nantucket, where he served as keeper from 1934 to 1937. Frank Grieder's last tour of duty as a light keeper was at the Gay Head Light from 1937 to 1948.

The following story about living at the Gay Head Light is in Bill Grieder's own words. This story was previously published in *Lighthouse Digest*, one of the world's leading lighthouse magazines, and is reprinted here with permission of its founder/publisher, Timothy Harrison.

IN THE WORDS OF BILL GRIEDER

When we left Great Point in '37, we were told the boat was going to pick us up. So all the furniture went down to the beach, and we sat there all day, all that night. We finally got a telegram that it had been delayed for a couple of weeks. So all the furniture had to go back up to the house and we had to wait for the lighthouse tender.

When we went to Gay Head we had a tarred road right to the front door. That really thrilled my Mum, to think she didn't have to go out in the sand.

They had a caretaker out at No Man's Land, and he got a bug. He signaled that he needed some assistance, so the Coast Guard went over. And he had to go to the hospital. They had a cow there, and the cow had to be milked twice a day. So the Coast Guard went over morning and night to milk the cow. I used to go with them the days when I wasn't in school. They used to call them the dairymaids. That didn't go over too well.

One night at Gay Head we had a nor'easter. I heard a plane going around. I ran out of the house—I could hear the plane flying and I could see the lights. It went around three of four times. It was a miserable night. The plane crashed that night at Lobsterville, just a mile down from the lighthouse. They came in to make a landing—they had their gear down. It hit a sand bar or something and it killed two pilots. I knew something was wrong. Evidently they were using the light to try to get a position.

A freighter came ashore halfway between the Devil's Bridge and the Gay Head Cliffs. And the Navy used it for bombing practice. They used smoke bombs. It was quite something.

There was always some work for me. I used to polish brass. I learned to light the lighthouse, and I taught my mother to do it. There were times when my Dad was sick—my Mum would go up to light the light or I would go up. Of course we had an assistant keeper, but if you couldn't call on him you did it yourself.

I went up to help whitewash or paint the tower, and mow the lawn of course. Lug the kerosene up in the tower. Polish the lens. Gay Head had 1,008 prisms. It had to be cleaned and dusted all the time. We had a dust cover over that (Fresnel lens). In the wintertime we used to put glycerin on the outside of the (lantern room) glass, so if you got rain it wouldn't ice up.

They used alcohol for the torches under the vaporizer for the lamp. They first used pure alcohol, and they had a run on alcohol. And it wasn't all going into the tower. The light wasn't the only thing that was being lit. So they switched to denatured alcohol. They had a sign on it: "POISON."

Another job I used to do was to take people up in the tower. My Mum used to do it too. We didn't have to do it but it was kind of a courtesy. Mostly anybody who stopped in we'd take them up.

One question they use to ask quite often is "Do you light the light on a foggy night?" I'd say, "Now you think what you just asked me. Suppose the fog clears up and the light is out." And they'd say they hadn't thought about that. That light is on every night. You could see it for 19 miles.

We had a generator coming supposedly to electrify Gay Head (Light). The Coast Guard was right next door to us. They had modern conveniences—plumbing, electricity, the works. We had outside privies and a pump. The commander of the Coast Guard was trying to get us these generators. Well, the 1938 hurricane came and the generators had to go to the Coast Guard to replace generators they had lost or something. There went our generators. The commander came down and he said, "Well, I'm still trying to get them for you." But he finally told us it was no use. My Mum said, "What do you think if I write to President Truman?" And he said, "Well, give it a try." So she wrote him saying, "In the '40s it's deplorable to have a station like this with no modern conveniences." He wrote back and he assured us that Gay Head would be electrified in the very near future. It was electrified, but my Dad had been retired when it was electrified.

Gay Head was a big, beautiful lighthouse. Well, that's history.

CHAPTER 11

THE LIGHTHOUSE LIBRARIES: SETTING THE STAGE FOR AMERICA'S LIBRARY SYSTEM

*When lonely, books help us escape—like taking a walk on a beach
when no school is nearby, lighthouse libraries help parents teach*

A LIGHTHOUSE KEEPER TEACHING AT GAY HEAD'S FIRST SCHOOL

The first confirmed schoolhouse in Gay Head existed in 1807. The "schoolhouse" was set up in the basement of the Baptist church and was described as "an apartment of stone called by no better than the cellar, in which, a school master keeps the Indian school. The winter season is the only part of the year in which it is kept…Some of his scholars are remarkably apt and the rest are not below the ordinary level."

The first teacher at this school was Gay Head Light keeper Ebenezer Skiff, who walked about a mile each day to teach at the one-room school. Before becoming a lighthouse keeper, Skiff lived in Chilmark with his family and worked as a part-time teacher and lawyer. Skiff's students at the first Gay Head School were capable of reading and speaking English, thanks to the religious teachings of preachers since the early 1700s and through comingling with colonists.

Besides teaching Wampanoag children, Skiff interacted with his neighbors by hiring local people to help maintain the wooden lighthouse's rotating light.

Ebenezer Skiff taught at the first Gay Head school in the basement of this Baptist church, circa 1806. *Author's collection.*

According to Hine's 1908 *Story of Martha's Vineyard*, during the early 1700s, one third of the Gay Head peninsula was controlled by London's "Society for Propagating the Gospel among the Indians and others in North America." These early Christian teachers used various religious texts to teach Wampanoag children to read and write English, thus giving Wampanoag children a foundation for understanding English when Ebenezer Skiff began teaching.

From 1807 until 1870, the Gay Head school system was financed and controlled by the state. During those sixty-three years, Gay Head natives were considered wards of the Commonwealth of Massachusetts and had an appointed commissioner to govern them.

GAY HEAD LIGHTHOUSE LIBRARY AND HOME SCHOOLING

While reading the Gay Head Lighthouse keeper's log, I came across an August 17, 1891 notation that read: "Steamer *Verbena* landed 2 corde of wood, paint, oil, turpentine and library."

Like a key unlocking a treasure-trove, the word "library" piqued my interest. Tapping into my Gay Head Light research, I found other references about a lighthouse library. My first assumption was that the lighthouse keepers gathered a bunch of books into a family library at their homes. As with any hidden treasure, I had to do some digging to uncover the riches.

I discovered that in 1848, the American Seaman's Friend Society (ASFS) began to furnish collections of books to crews of American ships. A branch of the ASFS was established in Boston under the name the Boston Seaman's Friend Society (BSFS). Under Madison Edwards of Falmouth, the BSFS initiated ministries and reading rooms in Woods Hole and Holmes Hole (Vineyard Haven).

As documented elsewhere in this book, Nantucket Sound and Vineyard Sound were the second-busiest waterways in the world (the English Channel being first). Holmes Hole had more commercial ships visiting its harbor than any New England port other than Boston. Thus, sailors rescued from wrecked ships or debarking and awaiting transfer to other ships found themselves ashore with few, if any, friends; little money; and in need of shelter and food.

It was for this reason that the Seaman's Bethel in Vineyard Haven was established to help provide temporary shelter, food and sustenance to needy sailors. However, the basis of this support system included a religious agenda.

A CAPTIVE SHIP AUDIENCE AND PROTESTANT LITERATURE

Besides helping wayward seaman, the Boston Seaman's Friend Society also served as a proselytizing tool for Protestant beliefs. A quote from the society's 1853 annual report states:

> *Commerce has always been the bone and sinew of national success. Two-thirds of the commerce of the world is in the hands of the Anglo-Saxon race; and the Protestants of the world, and its commanding influence, is being felt upon every ocean, river and sea. Hence the necessity that Christian principles should go in every ship, that the Protestant religion may stand side by side with Protestant thrift and enterprise.*

The American Seaman's Friend Society's agenda of distributing reading materials to sailors on merchant ships and at bethels eventually served as a model for America's newly formed U.S. Lighthouse Board.

FOUNDING OF THE LIGHTHOUSE LIBRARY SYSTEM

In 1852, the U.S. Lighthouse Board became the governmental successor to the U.S. Light House Establishment. The U.S. Lighthouse Board's 1875 annual report recommended distribution of reading materials to keepers because "by so doing, keepers will be made happier and more contented with their lot, and less desirous of absenting themselves from their post."

In 1876, the U.S. Lighthouse Board began distributing portable libraries to remote lighthouses via its fleet of lighthouse tender ships. The lighthouse library books were packed in specially designed wooden trunks with shelves. When a lighthouse keeper and his or her family were finished with a box of library materials, the keeper returned the library to a visiting tender ship in exchange for a new library. The wooden library cases, along with other lighthouse support materials, were transported to and from lighthouses about every three months.

In the late 1800s, there were more lighthouses than libraries in America, thus giving an assist to educating lighthouse keepers and their families. The double doors of each wooden library box swung outward to the left and right, allowing visible display of the titles on the spines of the books. A list of the reading materials was attached on the inside of the left door, while the right door displayed a list of the lighthouses the case

Portable lighthouse library crates were filled with reading materials and rotated to hundreds of lighthouse families. *Author's collection.*

had previously visited. Each case had a large identifying number burned into the exterior of the box to allow for tracking by the U.S. Lighthouse Board in Washington, D.C. These libraries continued to sustain a degree of Protestant religious influence.

In the February 1885 issue of the *Library Journal*, an article entitled "Lighthouse Libraries" by Arnold B. Johnson reads, in part:

> *Out of our seven hundred and fifty-five lighthouses and twenty-two lightships, fully one-third have each a library of about fifty volumes. The case for the books is so arranged that it "has a double debt to pay." Let it be shut, locked, and laid on its back, and it is a brassbound packing-case, with hinged handles by which it may be lifted; stand it on a table and open its doors, and it becomes a neat little bookcase, two shelves high, each twenty-one inches long, one adapted to hold ten octavos of the size of a bound volume of the "Century," and the other the right height for holding good-sized twelvemos* [books about five by seven and a half inches]. *As a matter of fact, many of these cases contain on the lower shelf ten volumes of bound magazines, and on the upper a judicious selection of biography, history, popular science, and good novels—from twenty-five to thirty volumes, according to thickness. A little space above the second shelf, about an inch and a half high, is utilized on one side by a copy of the New Testament, with Psalms, the octavo pica edition of the Bible Society, and on the other by the octavo edition of the Prayer Book, with hymnal attached, published by the Protestant Episcopal Publishing Society, but now out of print, as the Lighthouse Establishment took up the remainder of the edition.*

Similar to today's public library system, the U.S. Lighthouse Board had a system of tracking the readers of each book. This was done to help the board decide which books to keep in circulation and which to discard. Just as in our modern libraries, if a book was lost or damaged, there was a system of accountability. Each library contained a small blank book in which, according to Johnson, the

> *name of each reader is entered at the top of a page, and under his name is entered the title of each book he takes out, and the date it is taken and returned. The case is examined by the Lighthouse Inspector on his quarterly round, and its condition is reported. Any reader who loses or injures a book is required to replace it, if possible, in kind, and it is one of the rules that*

This artistic sticker placed inside the library crate's door identifies federal ownership. *Author's collection.*

the books shall not be lent from the stations, so that none but actual residents of lighthouses and lightships, the keepers and their families, shall have the use of them.

The U.S. lighthouse library program survived and thrived for thirty years and was well received by keepers and their families.

By 1885, there were 420 portable libraries serving U.S. lighthouses and lightships, including the Gay Head Light.

CHAPTER 12

MYSTERIOUS DEATHS AT THE GAY HEAD LIGHT

*One by one, each child died inside the dark smelly house
cause of death remains unknown—in the end, a family undone*

SICKNESS AND DEATH FROM 1890 TO 1907

In 1853, lighthouse keeper Samuel Flanders leaked news to the *Vineyard Gazette* that a new brick lighthouse was soon to be constructed to accommodate a first-order Fresnel lens. Along with the lighthouse came the construction of a new two-family keeper's house, also made of brick.

Previously, the lighting mechanism in the octagonal wooden lighthouse (1799–1856) required only one keeper to maintain the signal. The new first-order Fresnel lens had machinery that was much more complex and required the attention of at least two light keepers working in shifts.

In 1854, construction began on the new brick tower and the new two-family brick keeper's house. The keeper's house was constructed on the east side of the lighthouse. In 1856, Samuel Flanders and his family moved from their old wooden house into the new brick keeper's dwelling. This brick keeper's house was physically connected to the lighthouse by a narrow passageway for convenient access in any weather. The passageway was located in the middle of the two-family keeper's dwelling so that both the principal keeper and assistant keeper could conveniently access the lighthouse.

Above: A circa 1829 hand-painted woodcut of the 1799 Gay Head Light by Mrs. Edward Hitchcock. This is the first-ever color illustration of the Gay Head Cliffs. *Author's collection.*

Left: Oxcarts transport tourists from the steamship wharf to the lighthouse, circa 1885. Taking the steamer, with its live band music, to the lighthouse and cliffs was considered an upscale event. *Author's collection.*

Opposite: Two oxcarts with excursionists, circa 1885. The brick keeper's house, lighthouse and brownstone balcony appear painted. *Author's collection.*

Right: An 1885 postcard advertisement capitalizing on the 1884 wreck of *City of Columbus*. This card shows the *City of Columbus* with the Gay Head Light and Cliffs in the background. *Author's collection.*

Below: A panoramic view of Gay Head Cliffs and Gay Head Light looking north from the beach, circa 1920. *Author's collection.*

Compliments of the CLARK'S COVE GUANO CO. NEW BEDFORD, MASS.

GAY HEAD LIGHT, showing the Wreck of the "CITY OF COLUMBUS" Jan. 1884.

Presented by A. A. MITCHELL, General Agent, Portland, Maine.

Above: Large multi-level steamboats brought hundreds of passengers to enjoy daylong excursions to the Gay Head Light and Cliffs, circa 1892. This wharf was first constructed in 1883 and delivered tourists from New England ports. *Author's collection.*

Left: In this circa 1895 image, the lighthouse may or may not have been whitewashed. Many lighthouses were whitewashed to prevent salt spray and freezing water from infiltrating the mortar joints and weakening the structure. *Author's collection.*

Oxcarts driven by Wampanoag natives transport tourists to Gay Head Light from the steamboat wharf, circa 1895. *Author's collection.*

In this circa 1903 image, the lighthouse and nearby shed appear to be whitewashed. Rain barrels collect roof runoff water. *Author's collection.*

Above: Visitors enjoying the lighthouse and Vanderhoop Restaurant (right), circa 1909. The buildings located nearest to the right are his-and-her outhouses. *Author's collection.*

Left: Steamboat excursionists enjoy a day's outing, circa 1905. The lighthouse appears to be painted. *Author's collection.*

Steamboat wharf with nearby Pavilion dance and dining hall, circa 1890. The stable barn can be seen in the far distance, and the Pavilion can be seen in the foreground. *Author's collection*.

Gay Head Light at night, circa 1936. Notice Coast Guard Station Gay Head and its lookout tower to the left. *Author's collection*.

Gay Head Light and keeper's house, circa 1915. The lighthouse and its balcony appear to be painted with red clay paint. *Author's collection*.

View of the lighthouse from the northerly side, circa 1915. The lighthouse and keeper's house appear painted the same color, while the outbuildings appear to be whitewashed. Vanderhoop Restaurant can be seen in the far distance behind the oil shed at far right. *Author's collection.*

A view of the lighthouse and Vanderhoop Restaurant from the south side of the cliff, circa 1915. To the far left is the oil house, which was used to store kerosene to fire the Fresnel lens. *Author's collection.*

From 1799 to about 1915, oxcart transportation was an important aspect of island life. Improved roads for automobiles eventually replaced oxcarts and horse-powered modes of transport. *Author's collection.*

Gay Head Lighthouse. Marthas Vineyard. Mass.

Gay Head Light at night, circa 1948. Note the artistic placement of the ocean to the east side of the light. *Author's collection.*

A circa 1930 image showing the lighthouse, keeper's house and barn. Vanderhoop Restaurant can be seen between the lighthouse and the road, and the Not-A-Way Inn and Restaurant is to the right. *Author's collection.*

A circa 1952 watercolor illustrating the scenic Gay Head Cliffs, the lighthouse and recreation. *Author's collection.*

Above, left: These handmade crystal prisms of the 1854 Fresnel lens won a gold medal at the 1855 World's Fair. The Gay Head Light's initial white flash signal was often confused with the white flash of Nantucket's Sankaty Light, so in 1874 these ruby red glass panels were placed on the outside of the lens to create a "white, white, white, and red" signal. *Author's photo.*

Above, right: Exterior view of the clear glass prisms that from 1856 to 1874 emitted a constant series of white flashes without interruption of the red panels. *Author's photo.*

Above: Anna Carringer, assistant curator at Martha's Vineyard Museum, cleans and polishes a bulls-eye of the Fresnel. One must be careful not to cut his or her hands on the sharp prisms. *Author's photo*.

Opposite, bottom: Bulls-eye circles magnified the Fresnel lens light. When aligned with a sailor's line of vision, each bulls-eye appeared as a flash. *Author's photo*.

Above: View from the upstairs balcony facing south, November 2013. The cleared land in the middle of the photo is the center of the Gay Head circle by the cliff shops. *Author's photo*.

Opposite page, clockwise from top left: Side view of cast-iron sections with different shapes of the 1,008 handmade crystal prisms. The interior edge is sharp, while the exterior edge is wider. These prisms bend, magnify and concentrate the light's signal for up to twenty miles. *Author's photo*; There are fifty-one steps from the ground floor to the lantern room. These cast-iron steps were installed in 1900 and replaced the narrower 1854 stairs. Daylight brought in through the window assists in safe navigation. *Author's photo*; Mounted on a round platform is the pedestal and chariot for rotating the Fresnel lens. The brass clockwork used to turn the light can be seen behind the platform. A heavy weight was manually raised to generate mechanical energy. *Author's photo*; The custom cast-iron staircase and mahogany handrail were made to fit the curvature of the brick walls. *Author's photo*.

Lantern room view of the clay cliffs overlooking deadly Devil's Bridge and the Elizabeths. *Author's photo*.

An ethereal sunset on October 14, 2013—the same evening that tribal member Erick (Ricky) Vanderhoop died. Some family members felt that his spirit was expressing itself in this unusual configuration of clouds. *Author's photo*.

Tourists from a steamship visit the Gay Head Light, 1887. In this photograph, the lighthouse appears painted, and the whale-shaped weathervane indicates the absence of a lightning rod. Lightning strikes were common. *Martha's Vineyard Museum.*

The new brick keeper's house sat low to the ground and was supported by a shallow foundation anchored several feet below the surface into the clay and surrounding shallow layer of topsoil. The Flanders family resided in the new brick dwelling for eight years. In the twenty-nine years that followed, several families of principal and assistant keepers lived in the brick two-family dwelling without any reports of unusual illnesses.

This all changed in 1890, when the newly appointed principal keeper, William Atchison, took command and soon after fell ill. Atchison resigned in February 1891 due to illness and was replaced by Edward P. Lowe. Keeper Lowe quickly fell ill and died within one year. He died with his family in attendance inside his section of the two-family keeper's house at age forty-four. Lowe's death was noted in the 1892 Gay Head Light keeper's log simply as "Keeper died."

The next day, on February 20, the keeper's log noted: "Crosby L. Crocker assumed charge as Principle [*sic*] Keeper of Gay Head Light Station."

There was only room for two families at the Gay Head Light's two-family residence, which was basically two homes separated by a wall of bricks. Since it was imperative that the lighthouse be constantly manned by a full-time crew of physically able keepers, the Lowe family had to promptly vacate. The incoming keeper, Crosby Crocker, had a family with five members, and they needed all the rooms in their section of the dwelling.

A notation in the keeper's log dated February 20, 1892, just one day after the death of Keeper Lowe, states, "Mr. Lowe's Family left Station to day." One can only imagine the stress and sadness experienced by the Lowe family. It is assumed that Edward Lowe's body was placed in a wagon and either carted to a nearby cemetery or down to the dock at Pilot's Landing for transport via boat down island.

The nearby Pilot's Landing dock had been built by steamboat company investors in 1883 and served as a landing area for bringing tourists to visit the Gay Head Light and the Wampanoag natives. February certainly was not a month for tourists to visit Gay Head, so it is likely that the steamboats were not running and Lowe's family accompanied his body on a horse-drawn wagon.

SIX CHILDREN DIE WITHIN NINE YEARS

According to a historical document written in ink on lined paper, Crosby and Eliza Crocker had three children prior to moving into the Gay Head Light keeper's house in February 1892. The three children and their birth dates are as follows: Addie F. Crocker, born on December 8, 1886; James R. Crocker, born on August 11, 1887; and Marion C. Crocker, born on September 30, 1891. Based on this information, the ages of the three Crocker children when they moved into the Gay Head Light keeper's house in 1892 would have been: Addie, six years old; James, five years old; and Marion, one year old.

Once settled into the Gay Head Light keeper's house, Crosby and Eliza had three more children: George Herbert Crocker, born on January 21, 1892; Jannie J. Crocker, born on December 29, 1892; and Ruth Crocker, born on April 12, 1897.

By 1907, all six of the Crocker children would be dead.

Addie died at age eight on September 19, 1895; Marion died at age four on May 15, 1896; Jannie died at age three on May 26, 1896; James died

A circa 1895 image of what may be Keeper Crosby Crocker with members of his family. Six of the Crocker children died mysterious deaths. *Martha's Vineyard Museum.*

at age ten on July 27, 1898; Ruth died at age two on January 6, 1901; and George died at age fifteen on May 27, 1907.

There is no mention of funeral services or rituals for any of the deceased children, nor is there any mention as to how and where their bodies were buried. The occurrence of the deaths of the Crocker children on the lighthouse premises did little to deter the keepers from fulfilling their required duties. The rules of the U.S. Lighthouse Service were very demanding. Should a keeper become unable to fulfill his required tasks, he was promptly removed. Such strict regulations were necessary to protect the thousands of lives aboard the hundreds of vessels that each day used the Gay Head Light as an aid to navigation.

One of the many daily tasks required of a light keeper was maintaining the keeper's log.

GAY HEAD LIGHT KEEPER'S LOG

The Gay Head Light keeper's log kept a daily record of weather, shipwrecks, drownings, the comings and goings of visitors and lighthouse inspectors and the labors of the keepers. The Gay Head Light keeper's log is a hardcover book with lined pages that are about legal size in length and width. When you open the keeper's log, you see two facing pages. The page on the left recorded the weather for each day, and the page on the right recorded notations regarding maintenance of the lighthouse; shipwrecks and ship groundings on shoals; names and origins of ships and the size of their tour groups; supply deliveries; comings and goings of keepers, inspectors and guests; and the deaths of keepers and their family members.

In May 1896, the Gay Head Light keeper's log, for which Crosby Crocker was responsible, contained the following notations on the right-hand page:

May 1—Marion [Mammie] *taken sick to day Scarlet feaver*
May 2—Took the Stove down in the Watch room
May 3—George taken sick with Scarlet feaver
May 4—Changed The Reservoy & Cleaned the Burner
May 9—Jannie taken sick with Scarlet feaver
May 15—Mammie died to day at 11 am
May 17—Commenced Painting in the Tower
May 26—Jannie died to day at 8:30 am
May 29—Whitewashed the Barns
May 30—Finished Painting the Tower

It should be noted that the cause of illness of the above three children is recorded as "Scarlet feaver."

Whatever the cause of death, it was neither quick nor painless. Marion (Mammie) Crocker fell sick on May 1 and did not die until May 15. In other words, this four-year-old girl suffered for fourteen days in horrible pain, probably suffering through bouts of writhing delirium and loud crying episodes before dying.

A similar torturous death was suffered by Jannie Crocker, who was three years old when she fell ill on May 9. This little girl wrestled with death for seventeen days before dying on May 26.

In the midst of all this illness and death, the Gay Head Light keepers continued to faithfully fulfill their duties. Even though this may seem cold-hearted to some people, it is probably difficult for many of us to fathom how such grief of illness and death was managed 120 years ago. We must also keep in mind that the Gay Head Light was a remote outpost separated by a one- or two-day horseback journey to the nearest town. In other words, no doctors were readily available.

Marion taken sick to day scarlet feaver
Took the Stove down in the watch room
George taken sick with scarlet feaver
Changed The Kerosway. & cleaned. The Burner

Jannie taken sick to day scarlet feaver

Mammie died to day at 11 am

commenced Painting in the Tower

Janie died to day at 8.30 am

Whitewashed the Barn
finished Painting the Tower

Entries in the lighthouse logbook made by Keeper Crocker in 1896. May 1—Marion (Mammie) falls ill; May 3—George falls ills; May 9—Jannie falls ill; May 15—Marion dies; May 26—Jannie dies. *Martha's Vineyard Museum.*

It is also possible that due to the high rate of infant mortality during that era, death might not have been as traumatic as it sometimes can be today. Perhaps a sort of emotional distance had to be maintained for psychological and emotional survival.

On another note, it seems almost unimaginable that as the three Crocker children lay dying and suffering in their beds, all resources were not devoted to giving the children attention and physical relief. Certainly, there was a need for maintaining the Fresnel light as an aid to navigation. However, commencing with "Painting the Tower" just two days after Mammie's death and while her sister Jannie lay dying – makes one wonder. And, just two days after Jannie dies – the keepers are out there whitewashing the barns and painting the tower.

No mention is made of any ceremony or mourning process taking place, nor is there any mention of how the bodies were disposed.

UNITED STATES LIFE-SAVING SERVICE INSPECTS THE KEEPER'S HOUSE

In 1899, the United States Life-Saving Service inspected and reported on the condition of the keeper's house:

> *Gay Head, Martha's Vineyard, Massachusetts,—The double dwelling occupied by the keeper and his assistant, with their families, is of brick. Its floor is at a level with the ground, and prevents the raising of the grade to turn water from the clay site. Rain driven against the walls and running down them into the ground is retained by the impervious soil, and keeps the cellars and unexcavated ground under the building and the lower rooms so damp that mold and mildew gather on the walls of the rooms and on household articles. The eaves are but nine feet from the ground, and the upper rooms are too low and ill-lighted for convenient use. The house is too damp and unsanitary for safe occupation by human beings. It is estimated that it can be rebuilt, at a cost not exceeding $6,500, and the Board recommends that an appropriation of this amount be made therefore.*

News of the mysterious deaths of the Crocker children at the Gay Head Lighthouse quickly spread across the island and through the U.S. Lighthouse

Service. Four days after the death of the Crockers' fifth child, two-year-old Ruth, on January 6, 1901, Keeper Crocker received the following handwritten letter dated January 10, 1901:

> *Mr. Crocker*
>
> *Please fill the inclosed* [sic] *blanks, and if you will send me the dates of the deaths of all the children you have lost, I would like to see if all are recorded in this town.*
>
> *Yours truly,*
> *Wm. S. Swift, Town Clerk of Tisbury*

One can only imagine the mindset of Crosby and Eliza Crocker as they sat down at a table to fill in the requested blanks to record the births and deaths of their children.

On a related note, two weeks later, on January 23, 1901, the Crockers received the following handwritten letter from a lighthouse official who was serving on board the U.S. Lighthouse Service tender *Azalea*:

> *Dear Mr. Crocker,*
>
> *Has the drinking water at your Station been analyzed? It struck me that possibly it may have to do with the troubles that have proved so fatal to your children.*
>
> *If no examination has been made I will have one made in Boston if you will please pack up a bottle or tin of water carefully and put it in a box. Send it to the office, at the same time writing a letter to inform us that you have done so.*
>
> *I trust you will all very soon be enjoying better Health.*
>
> *Very truly yours,*
> *Arthur P. Nagro*

The *Azalea* was a lighthouse tender (ship) built in 1891 for the U.S. Lighthouse Service. The *Azalea* was located in the Second Light House District, which included Martha's Vineyard. Like all lighthouse tenders of that era, the *Azalea* was named after a flower and was specifically designed to help maintain, support and tend to lighthouses and light vessels. Lighthouse tender support included the shipping of supplies and fuel, transportation of keepers and U.S. Lighthouse Service personnel, managing the lighthouse library system and the provision of mail services.

Obviously, this letter from an officer of the U.S. Lighthouse Service to Crocker was an effort to help the Crocker family determine the cause of death of their five children. It was also an effort to try to determine if contaminated water had contributed to the deaths.

According to the Gay Head Light keeper's log, an inspection of the keeper's dwelling was made by the U.S. Lighthouse Board in September 1898. The following year, the U.S. Lighthouse Board reported that the house was "too damp and unsanitary for safe occupation by human beings" and recommended $6,500 for a new house. However, this determination did not come in time to save Ruth Crosby's life, who died at the age of two on January 6, 1901.

In 1902, the U.S. Lighthouse Board built a spacious gambrel-roofed, double dwelling constructed of wood. The foundation of the new keeper's

List of births and deaths of the Crocker children written in the logbook. *Martha's Vineyard Museum.*

house was purposely built higher off the ground. In 1902–03, Crosby Crocker; his wife, Eliza; and their only surviving child, George, moved into the newly constructed keeper's home. Crosby and Eliza Crocker continued to live and work at the Gay Head Light even after George's death in 1907.

A search of records provided no information about George's death. If he had contracted "Scarlet feaver" in 1896 along with his two sisters, it is possible that he suffered and died from complications of this disease. Complications from scarlet fever may include:

- rheumatic fever (an inflammatory disease that can affect the heart, joints, skin and brain)
- kidney disease (inflammation of the kidneys, called poststreptococcal glomerulonephritis)
- ear infections (otitis media)
- skin infections
- abscesses of the throat
- pneumonia (lung infection)
- arthritis (joint inflammation)

After thirty-four years as principal keeper of the Gay Head Lighthouse, Crosby L. Crocker retired in 1920. After leaving the Gay Head Light keeper's house, he and his wife, Eliza, relocated to the down-island town of Vineyard Haven.

ELIZA CROCKER'S OBITUARY AS PUBLISHED IN THE *VINEYARD GAZETTE*

When Eliza Crocker died in May 1929, her obituary made no mention of her predeceased children and only hinted at her life's sadness and hardships.

BORN ON NANTUCKET

Mrs. Crocker Was 34 Years at Gay Head Light

Mrs. Eliza C. Crocker, wife of Capt. Crosby L. Crocker of Vineyard Haven, died at the Martha's Vineyard Hospital on Saturday night, March 30, aged 68 years. Mrs. Crocker had been in poor health for several years, and had been particularly ill during the entire winter. She had just been removed to the hospital when she died.

Mrs. Crocker was born on Nantucket, her parents being James G. and Adaline Fisher. It was there that she met and married her husband, who was in the light-house service, and the couple lived on that island for two years when they came to the Vineyard. After two years at Oak Bluffs, Captain Crocker was transferred to Gay Head, and there he and his wife lived for thirty-four years.

When the captain retired nine years ago, the couple removed to Vineyard Haven, where they since remained.

Mrs. Crocker was a member of the Baptist Church, and was well known for the quiet fortitude which permitted her to find satisfaction in the isolated life she was forced to lead for many years.

Mrs. Crocker is survived by her husband; a brother, Alonzo D, Fisher; and a sister, Mrs. Arthur C. Manter, both of Nantucket.

Funeral services were held at her late home on Tuesday afternoon. Rev. Willard S. Jackson officiating. Burial was at Oak Grove Cemetery, Vineyard Haven.

CENTER FOR DISEASE CONTROL EVALUATES LIGHTHOUSE DEATHS

In its June 2006 report, "Mold Prevention Strategies and Possible Health Effects in the Aftermath of Hurricanes and Major Floods," the United States Centers for Disease Control and Prevention (CDC) stated that "excessive exposure to mold-contaminated materials can cause adverse health effects in susceptible persons regardless of the type of mold or the extent of contamination."

When mold spores are present in abnormally high quantities, they can present especially hazardous health risks to humans, including allergic reactions and poisoning or fungal infections caused by mycotoxins.

A mycotoxin—from the Greek μύκης (mykes, mukos), meaning "fungus," and τοξικόν (toxikon), meaning "poison"—is a toxic secondary metabolite produced by organisms of the fungi kingdom, commonly known as molds. The term "mycotoxin" is usually reserved for the toxic chemical products produced by fungi.

Most fungi are aerobic (requiring oxygen) and are found almost everywhere in extremely small quantities due to the minute size of their spores. They consume organic matter wherever humidity and temperature are sufficient. Where conditions are right, fungi proliferate into colonies, and mycotoxin levels become high.

The reason for the production of mycotoxins is unknown, as they are not necessary for the growth and/or development of the fungi. Because mycotoxins weaken the receiving host, the fungus might produce them as a strategy to create host bodies for further fungal proliferation.

The production of toxins depends on the surrounding environments, and the toxins vary greatly in their severity, depending on the organism infected and its susceptibility, metabolism and defense mechanisms. Some of the adverse health effects found in animals and humans include weakened immune systems, diseases and even death.

In early January 2014, I sent all the information I had about the deaths of the Crocker children to the CDC. The CDC replied with the following:

Dear Mr. Waterway:

Thank you for contacting the Centers for Disease Control and Prevention (CDC) with your inquiry.
The symptoms of scarlet fever are:

A very red, sore throat
A fever (101° F or above)
A red rash with a sandpaper feel
Bright red skin in underarm, elbow and groin creases
A whitish coating on the tongue or back of the throat
A "strawberry" tongue
Headache
Nausea or vomiting
Swollen glands
Body aches

The symptoms of mold exposure are nasal stuffiness, eye irritation, wheezing and/or skin irritation. Severe reactions may include fever and shortness of breath. Some people with chronic lung illnesses, such as obstructive lung disease, may develop mold infections in their lungs.

As indicated above, "skin irritation" and "fever" are symptoms found in both scarlet fever and mold exposure. This information might provide some clue about the deaths of the Crocker children.

Regardless, the mystery remains as to what actually killed Keeper Edward Lowe and the six Crocker children.

CAPTAIN CROSBY L. CROCKER: ALONE IN OLD AGE

Crosby Crocker's wife, Eliza, died on March 30, 1929.

In April 1929, a month after his wife's death, Crocker sat down with a reporter from the *Martha's Vineyard Gazette* and shared his life's story. Crocker's story was published by the *Gazette* on May 3, 1929.

The *Gazette* reporter described Crosby Crocker in this fashion: "For one who has seen so much sorrow and whose life has contained so many disappointments, Captain Crocker is surprisingly cheerful and an entertaining companion. A rugged, upright figure, with snowy hair and mustache, he looks the part of an old seafarer as he sits and smokes the pipe that solaces him in his loneliness."

The end of this lengthy *Gazette* article concludes with Crocker sharing his Gay Head Light story about the night of the November gale of 1898. At the time of this historic gale, Crocker's surviving family consisted of his wife, Eliza; his one-year-old daughter, Ruth; and his six-year-old son, George. I found it curious that while telling his story, Crocker never mentioned concern for the safety of his wife and two children, who were inside the keeper's house during the storm.

> *On the night of the November gale in 1898, which was the worst storm the captain ever saw, the light and his horse kept him fully occupied. He believed that his barn was about to blow down and for a time stood by ready to lead the horse out if the building started to crash. "You could see the ides weave in and out at every gust," he says.*
>
> *Up in the tower the draught nearly extinguished the light. The windows as tight as human skill could make them and the hatchway in the floor closed, the powerful lamp was dimmed until it scarcely showed. Not that it made much difference, for no vessel could have seen it in the smother of snow, rain and sleet.*

That was about the only time that the captain ever had to shovel snow around the lighthouse. Ordinarily it all blows over the cliff, but on that memorable occasion there was so much snow on the ground that paths had to be dug.

So the years passed, and nine years ago the captain and his wife left the Head, alone…and coming to Vineyard Haven lived there together until Mrs. Crocker passed away just a short time ago, leaving the captain to stand out the watch alone…

CHAPTER 13

LIGHTHOUSE MEDICINE

Before cutting off an arm to keep a patient from harm
cut a vein; let an arm's worth of blood into a bucket drain

To understand the practice of medicine at the Vineyard's lighthouses, one must embrace the local practice of medicine.

According to John Duffy's book *From Humors to Medical Science*, America's colonies were ravaged by starvation, malnutrition, poor sanitation, fever and disease. Over 80 percent of colonists in early Virginia died in their first years, and approximately 50 percent of the settlers in Massachusetts died during their first winter. Needless to say, the survival rate of patients treated with American medicine in the seventeenth and eighteenth centuries was dismal.

During the seventeenth, eighteenth and nineteenth centuries, homeopathy, hydrotherapy, herbal medicine (including marijuana) and bloodletting were all considered forms of "medicine."

In colonial years, midwifery was common on Martha's Vineyard, as most births occurred at home. In her article "All American Girl," Susan Norwood writes, "The women of colonial times were usually pregnant and caring for their young children. The second generation of colonial women had an average of about eight children. Childbirth was a fearful time for them. Death was an issue not to be dismissed with each birth. Childbirth was a communal affair attended by midwives and neighboring women."

While researching my book *The Holy Order of Water: Healing Earth's Waters and Ourselves*, I learned of the high mortality rate of women and their babies during the eighteenth and nineteenth centuries. A major cause of death was germs spread by unwashed hands of attending midwives and doctors. As early as 1843, Dr. Oliver Wendell Holmes proposed washing hands. During his visits to American hospitals, Holmes observed that death by so-called childbed fever was greatly reduced where hand washing was practiced. Holmes was horrified by the prevalence in American hospitals of the childbed fever, which he believed to be some kind of illness passed to pregnant women and their babies by the hands of doctors and midwives. At the time, the concept of "germs" was unknown. After sharing his theory with the American medical establishment, Holmes was chastised by several leading American orthodox obstetricians for proposing such a ridiculous idea.

In addition to caring for people, doctors also cared for farm animals—a frightening scenario when you consider doctors tending to farm animals and then tending to people without washing their hands.

On a similar note, when tooth extraction, amputation or surgery were practiced during the seventeenth and eighteenth centuries and even into the early nineteenth century, all were accomplished without anesthesia or painkillers. Morphine wasn't available until the mid-1800s. During the amputation process, doctors and nurses did not wash their hands or sanitize their garments or medical tools. In fact, some doctors wore their unwashed, bloodstained, germ-filled aprons as a symbol of experience. It is for these reasons that hospitalization often exposed people to a realm rife with infectious diseases and deadly bacteria. Due to lack of knowledge of germs, the doctors themselves became primary vectors of disease and infection.

Bloodletting was a form of medicine widely accepted by doctors and practitioners in Europe and America. In fact, the local barber used the same straight razor for shaving clients that he used for cutting veins to let blood flow into a bucket. Barbara R. Carter's 2005 book, *Childbed Fever*, states:

> *One British medical text recommended bloodletting for acne, asthma, cancer, cholera, coma, convulsions, diabetes, epilepsy, gangrene, gout, herpes, indigestion, insanity, jaundice, leprosy, ophthalmia, plague, pneumonia, scurvy, smallpox, stroke, tetanus, tuberculosis, and some one hundred other diseases. Bloodletting was even used to treat most forms of hemorrhaging such as nosebleed, excessive menstruation, or hemorrhoidal bleeding. Before surgery or at the onset of childbirth, blood was removed to prevent inflammation. Before amputation, it was customary to remove a quantity of blood equal to the amount believed to circulate in the limb that was to be removed.*

When the Gay Head Lighthouse was located on the west end of Martha's Vineyard, there was no hospital on island. The only care for the people of Gay Head was usually their time-tested homegrown remedies. It would be about one hundred years before Gay Head was to see minimal access to evolving medicine.

However, due to the nature of its location down island, the need for medicine at Homes Hole was critical. Many island people petitioned for a hospital in Homes Hole to address the contagious diseases landed by crews sailing the Atlantic. In 1822, the town voted to "Petition Congress to Erect a Hospital in This Town for the Reception of Distressed Seamen or Make Some Provision for Seamen That May be Landed Here Destitute of the Means of Support."

Decades went by with unsatisfactory results. Finally, in 1879, the abandoned Homes Hole lighthouse, located at the head of the harbor, was converted into a hospital. During the time of conversion, the U.S. Lighthouse Establishment transferred ownership of the buildings and grounds for hospital use.

According to Charles Banks's *Annals of Tisbury*:

> *It* [the lighthouse] *was opened on Nov. 28, 1879, under the charge of Acting Assistant Surgeon W.D. Stewart of the general service, and became a marine hospital and a station of the first class officially. This officer* [Stewart], *who had greatly endeared himself to the community through a period of seven years, died October 30, 1886, and was succeeded temporarily by Assistant Surgeon Seaton Norman, and later as a regular detail by Passed Assistant Surgeon R.P.M. Ames (1886–1889). From this time forward the hospital has been under command of regularly commissioned officers…*

GAY HEAD LIGHT MEDICINE

Throughout the 1800s and early 1900s, Gay Head residents had little access to medical care. Most families continued to rely on their use of native herbal remedies, rituals and healing medicine man traditions.

Wampanoag tribal leader Gladys Widdiss remembers that during the 1920s, it took a Vineyard Haven doctor from to three to five hours to travel to Gay Head—weather permitting. According to Gladys, most of the tribal members continued to use the herbal remedies passed down for generations.

It is for these reasons that we understand why there is no mention of a doctor having tended to the children who died at the Gay Head Light in the 1890s—even though it is a matter of record that it took up to two weeks for two of the children to die. At the time, the practicing doctor in Vineyard Haven was Winthrop Butler, who served as an island doctor from 1867 until he suffered a stroke in 1903.

The fact that the Crocker children died from what was diagnosed as "Scarlet feaver" might indicate that there was no known cure or way to treat scarlet fever in the late nineteenth century.

During the 1890s, when the Crocker children were dying from scarlet fever, the Martha's Vineyard Marine Hospital was fully operational. Also, there was a Vineyard Haven doctor available for visitation and care of the dying children at the Gay Head Light. Why is there is no mention of a physician tending to the dying children? Why were the children not transported to the Martha's Vineyard Marine Hospital? Perhaps the sad answer is that the dying children were considered helpless cases.

CHAPTER 14

HISTORY OF BUILDINGS
NEAR THE GAY HEAD LIGHT

Travelers from afar came to see clay cliffs, natives and "the Light";
restaurants, shops and boardinghouses soon occupied the site

UNITED STATES LIFE-SAVING SERVICE BUILDING

Located north of the Gay Head Light, the lookout building was constructed circa 1879 by the Massachusetts Humane Society. The U.S. Life-Saving Service took over the site in 1885 and constructed a new building and lookout tower, as well as a new boathouse along the nearby shore of Dogfish Bar. If an emergency were sighted from the lookout tower, the rescue crew would run down to the boathouse and launch their rescue boat from Dogfish Bar beach.

In 1895, the newly formed U.S. Coast Guard took over all United State Life-Saving Service stations and their affiliated boathouses. The site of the lookout tower and its related buildings was renamed Coast Guard Station Gay Head.

During the late 1940s, the U.S. Coast Guard relocated its Gay Head station and boat rescue operations to the Menemsha Harbor area. In 1952, the U.S. Coast Guard physically abandoned the Coast Guard Station Gay Head, and in 1953, it demolished and removed all the buildings.

The U.S. Life-Saving Station north of the lighthouse, circa 1896. Gay Head's lifesaving station was manned mostly by Wampanoags. The lighthouse appears whitewashed in the background of this photo. *Martha's Vineyard Museum.*

U.S. Life-Saving Service boathouse at Dogfish Bar beach, circa 1896. The crew would run from the station to the beach and launch their rescue boat. *Martha's Vineyard Museum.*

In this circa 1884 photo of steamship tourists, the lighthouse appears to be painted. *Martha's Vineyard Museum.*

THE BRICK KEEPER'S HOUSE (1856–1902)

The brick lighthouse keeper's house was constructed in 1856 to replace the wooden structure that had served as the keeper's house for the wooden Gay Head Light. This brick keeper's house was completed in 1856 along with the new brick Gay Head Light to accommodate a first-order Fresnel lens. This brick keeper's house was attached to the lighthouse by an enclosed access way.

In 1902, the brick keeper's house was torn down and replaced by a larger, two-story keeper's house. This keeper's house was torn down and replaced after the mysterious deaths of a lighthouse keeper and another keeper's five children.

VANDERHOOP RESTAURANT (LATE 1800s–CIRCA 1935)

The Vanderhoop Restaurant was built by Charles W. Vanderhoop Sr.'s mother and stepfather in the late 1800s. It was built near the Gay Head Light on the south side of the property between the lighthouse and the Gay Head Cliffs overlook.

Charles Vanderhoop Sr. and his brother, Bert, bought the Vanderhoop Restaurant from their parents in the early 1900s. According to Leonard Vanderhoop, the Vanderhoop Restaurant had eight to ten tables and featured a specialty of lobster dinners. Business was brisk during the summers—especially on weekends, when the steamships were in.

Charles Vanderhoop Sr. sold his interest in the restaurant to his brother when Bert married. To local people, the restaurant became known as Bert's Restaurant. The Vanderhoop Restaurant is often visible in vintage Gay Head Light postcards from that era. The Vanderhoop Restaurant burned down in the 1930s.

According to Ann Vanderhoop, the existing Vanderhoop Restaurant overlooking the ocean near the cliffs' viewing area was built in the early 1940s by Napoleon Bonaparte Madison. Eventually, Luther Madison and Ann took over the ownership of the restaurant. To help bring business to the restaurant, the family installed a cliff trail from the restaurant down to the beach. The trail, called the Bunny Trail, made it convenient for people to access the clay cliffs beach and to walk up to the restaurant for lunch or sunset dinners.

Victoria Haeselbarth at the "Bunny Trail to Beach" sign, 1968. Tourists used this path as beach access from the Vanderhoop Restaurant. *Courtesy Diane Haeselbarth.*

NOT-A-WAY HOUSE (CIRCA 1918–CIRCA 1970)

According to Helen Manning, the Not-A-Way House was built around 1918 by an off-island man from New Bedford named Gennochio. The first floor featured a large dining room with a kitchen. The upstairs had about six bedrooms for family and guests. Since there was no running water or indoor plumbing, all guesthouses in Aquinnah used chamber pots for sanitation up until the early 1950s. The Not-A-Way also offered two nearby outhouses—one for men and one for women.

Like those in the Vanderhoop Restaurant's dining room, the dining room windows of the Not-A-Way capitalized on the view of the ocean along the shore facing Nomans Land Island. The dining room also featured several cages of canaries scattered in different locations so as to fill the room with birdsong.

As with the families living at the Gay Head Light and owners of other Gay Head restaurants and guesthouses, the drinking water for patrons at the Not-A-Way came from water at the mile-distant Cook's Spring. Like most other restaurants and guesthouses, the Not-A-Way was a seasonal business and closed during the off-season. Helen Manning's parents managed the Not-A-Way, and Helen worked there doing various jobs such as waitressing, gardening, chamber maid work and fetching water. The Not-A-Way had a large garden located in the area that now serves as the town parking lot at the circle.

Over time, the Not-A-Way deteriorated to the point that it stood as an abandoned and dangerous eyesore. According to Bettina Washington, the Wampanoag tribal historic preservation officer, the town voted for the Gay Head Fire Department to burn down the Not-A-Way and its outhouses before the town's centennial in 1970.

KEEPER'S HOUSE (1902–1962)

The wooden, gambrel-roof keeper's house at the Gay Head Light was constructed in 1901 and finished in 1902. It replaced the brick keeper's residence that had been the scene of a series of illnesses and deaths. It was designed as a two-family house to accommodate the principal keeper, the assistant keeper and their respective families. It was a photogenic keeper's house that complemented the Gay Head Light. The house was without

A rare image of the keeper's house being razed, circa 1961. The white pile might be plaster from the inside walls of the lighthouse. The brick pile at the far left is rubble from the razed U.S. Coast Guard tower. *Courtesy Margaret DeWolf.*

indoor plumbing and bathrooms until 1953, when it was electrified, and never had potable water from an onsite well. Drinking water available only at the mile-distant Cook's Spring. This building was demolished along with the brick U.S. Coast Guard tower in 1962–63.

U.S. COAST GUARD BRICK TOWER (CIRCA 1952–1962)

In the 1940s, the U.S. Coast Guard decided to demolish its Coast Guard Station Gay Head facility and move to a new facility at Menemsha. Due to its ready water access, the Menemsha location was already in use by the U.S. Coast Guard for search and rescue and quasi-military operations.

The Coast Guard Station Gay Head facility and its lookout tower were originally constructed in 1885 by the United State Life-Saving Service. In 1915, the newly formed U.S. Coast Guard took control of all U.S. Life-Saving Service lookout towers and buildings situated above the clay cliffs just north of the Gay Head Light.

In the late 1940s and early 1950s, the U.S. Coast Guard abandoned and razed its old lookout tower and related buildings at Coast Guard Station Gay Head.

The U.S. Coast Guard constructed its square brick lookout tower next to the Gay Head Light around 1952. The U.S. Coast Guard brick tower was demolished at the same time as the Gay Head Light's keeper's house around 1962.

Buddy Vanderhoop inspects the lookout room that came from the top of the U.S. Coast Guard tower. *Author's collection.*

The stairwell to the top of the U.S. Coast Guard brick tower was of open breezeway construction. The lookout room at the top of the tower was insulated and heated for year-round surveillance of Vineyard Sound. When the U.S. Coast Guard brick tower was demolished, the uppermost lookout room was preserved and transported about one mile to a private estate off Jeffer's Way. The lookout room of the old U.S. Coast Guard tower now serves as a modest guesthouse.

AQUINNAH HOUSE

In the late 1800s, Wampanoag Edwin DeVries Vanderhoop built a hotel called the Aquinnah House. This nineteen-room hotel was located on a hill overlooking the ocean southwest of the lighthouse. The ocean-facing section of the property contains a flagpole and daymark structure. Toward the end of its functional life, the Aquinnah House deteriorated to the point that it was no longer suitable as a guesthouse. For a while, it became known as the "Haunted House" before it was demolished.

The Aquinnah House, pictured here circa 1888, had nineteen rooms to accommodate visitors arriving by steamboat. *Author's collection.*

HELEN MANNING'S HOME AND RESTAURANT

In 1952, Helen Manning built her home on inherited land abutting the Gay Head Lighthouse property. Shortly afterward, Helen also built the nearby Manning Restaurant. Helen served as an assistant keeper from 1985 to 1990 and worked closely with VERI in curtailing vandalism of the lighthouse.

Current Wampanoag tribal chairman Tobias Vanderhoop recalls his childhood years living a short walk from the Manning restaurant. Tobias recalls saving his money so he could play video games at Manning's Restaurant. Due to the nearby location of his grandfather's home, Tobias harbors fond memories of lying in bed at night as the white, white, white and red flash of the light illuminated his bedroom window. "It was like having a rhythmic night light in my bedroom to help put me to sleep. The presence of the pulsing light was there every night—almost like a friend," said Tobias during an interview.

Lighthouse neighbor and assistant keeper Helen Manning (right) with friends. *Author's collection.*

THREE HISTORIC AERIAL IMAGES

Visible in this circa 1951 image are: the Fresnel lens, protected by drawn shade; the fuel shed (lower left); the outhouse; the keeper's house; the barn (right); the garden; the newly installed electric lines along the road; and the Not-A-Way Inn located across street. *Martha's Vineyard Museum.*

In this circa 1958 image, the U.S. Coast Guard brick tower is visible, but the fuel shed and outhouse have been removed. Also note the electric signal in the lighthouse lantern room, the abandoned garden and the recently vacated keeper's house, which has been boarded shut. *Author's collection.*

In this circa 1965 image, the disturbed, barren soil around the light gives testimony to the recently removed U.S. Coast Guard tower. To the left of the light is the Manning home and restaurant, and across the road is the Not-A-Way House with its his-and-her outhouses. *Author's collection.*

CHAPTER 15

FIGHT OVER THE FRESNEL

In 1954, Gay Head and Edgartown ended up in a schism
over the lens with 1,008 prisms, now it resides at the MV Museum

THE FIGHT OVER THE GAY HEAD FRESNEL

The Gay Head Fresnel lens was installed in 1856.

In 1950, the U.S. Coast Guard announced plans to "modernize" the Gay Head Light in the event that electricity was ever installed in the town. Without hesitation, the Boston Museum of Science contacted the Coast Guard and expressed interest in taking possession of the Gay Head Fresnel lens if that were to occur. Upon learning of this news, the Dukes County Historical Society submitted a letter of protest.

In 1951, electrification was well on its way to the town of Gay Head—the last town in Massachusetts to receive electricity. So, too, were plans by the U.S. Coast Guard to transfer the Gay Head Fresnel to Boston. Upon hearing of this news, the community of Martha's Vineyard made preparations to fight the good fight to keep the Fresnel lens on the island. Certainly, the island had its reasons:

1. The Fresnel lens was designed specifically for the brick tower above the Gay Head Cliffs.
2. The Fresnel lens had served gallantly in its purpose to save lives, its light having flashed across Vineyard Sound for almost one hundred years.

3. Over the many decades, the Fresnel lens had become part of the culture of Martha's Vineyard. It was deeply embedded in the island's poetry, songs, music, books, educational programs, museum exhibits, business and organizational logos and cultural events such as May Day.
4. The international identity of Martha's Vineyard was married to the presence of the Fresnel lens and its location above the scenic clay cliffs.
5. The Fresnel lens made a recognized contribution to the island's economy.

As in most cases when the island of Martha's Vineyard does battle with an off-island adversary, the community rallied as one.

Fortunately for Martha's Vineyard, the Boston Museum of Science also took an interest in the Navesink Fresnel bivalve optic. After successfully obtaining the Fresnel bivalve optic from Navesink, the Boston Museum of Science decided to relinquish its claim on the Gay Head Fresnel.

With a sigh of relief, Martha's Vineyard seemed assured to keep the Gay Head Fresnel on the island. However, this statement begged two questions:

1. Where on Martha's Vineyard would the Gay Head Fresnel be moved?
2. Which town or local organization would assume the financial and legal responsibility for taking care of the Gay Head Fresnel?

Thus, in June 1951, the battle over the Fresnel lens began.

Since museums speak similar language, the Dukes County Historical Society (DCHS) had been in contact with the Boston Museum of Science in an attempt to dissuade it from taking possession of the Gay Head Fresnel. Upon securing the Navesink Fresnel Lens, Bradford Washburn, director of the Boston Museum of Science, wrote a letter in June 1951 to DCHS president Gerald Chittenden: "The Museum of Science has secured a very fine light from Navesink, New Jersey, and it has been successfully installed in our new building. We therefore wish to exercise no special claim on Gay Head and wish you all luck in connection with your plans for moving it to the Dukes County Historical Society."

The U.S. Coast Guard's plan was to electrify and remove the Gay Head Fresnel during the summer of 1952. DCHS had little money in its coffers at the time, so it immediately launched a fundraising campaign to design and build a structure to house the Fresnel in Edgartown. Simultaneously, the Gay Head Improvement Association gathered forces in an effort to keep the Fresnel in Gay Head.

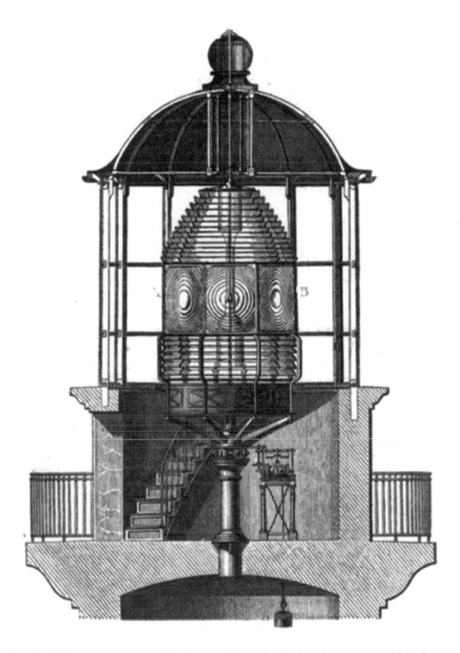

Profile of the lantern room and clock room below. The clockworks was powered by a heavy weight (lower center right) that turned the lens. *Author's collection.*

As reported in the *Martha's Vineyard Gazette* on March 7, 1952:

> *From the State House, it has been learned that the Gay Head Improvement Association, chartered as a corporation about forty years ago, is still a legally constituted organization. Accordingly, new officers were elected at a meeting held on Monday night, with Lorenzo D. Jeffers elected President; Capt. Walter W. Manning, Vice President; Miss Alberta Jeffers, treasurer; and Mrs. Luther Madison, clerk.*
>
> *Following the adjournment of the town meeting on Tuesday and while the voters were assembled, Mr. Jeffers took over the chair and explained the position of the association and asked for comment of any kind.*
>
> *It was agreed without dissent that membership in the association should be sought at once, both from native Islanders and others who may be interested, and that the public poll on sentiment regarding the location of the lens should be started immediately.*
>
> *It was brought out that in the poll held by the Association for the Advancement of Good Government, organized in the Down-Island towns, before the recent meeting was called by the Coast Guard, the result was better than ten to one in favor of enshrining the old lens in the town of Gay Head...A number of people spoke on the matter, all favoring a development of some consequence in the town of Gay Head if the lens can be located there. The suggestion has come from outside the township that the lens, if it remains in the town, should be exhibited in connection with an Indian museum. As the situation stands, Mr. Jeffers explained, three months have been allowed by the Coast Guard, at the end of which time the light will be dismantled and the lens removed. A place for its reception must have been decided upon by that time.*
>
> *It was indicated at this meeting that the Dukes County Historical Society will not consider any change in its original plan, that is, to enshrine the lens at Edgartown, and that unless this plan is followed, the society will have nothing to do with it.*

As can be imagined, the *Martha's Vineyard Gazette* was flooded with letters expressing positions on both sides. Many letters were emotionally charged and accusatory:

> *May I add that I too feel that the Gay Head Light lens belongs at Gay Head in its natural setting instead of becoming a curiosity in the center of a beautiful country village. A windmill would look as much out of place in Central Park.*
> *—Clinton P. West, Wilmington, Del.*

Tom and I want to add our protests to those already voiced, against the removal of the Gay Head Light to Edgartown. Surely, its years of service warrant it a more appropriate and familiar resting place than the end of a village street—without even a glimpse of water!

Vineyarders always put up a fight for the preservation of Island traditions, and those of us off-islanders who love the place feel just as strongly. A lighthouse belongs by the sea. Public protest in New York saved the Little Red Lighthouse under the George Washington Bridge. It is hoped that the same kind of public protest and loving concern will save the old Gay Head Light from retirement to the Historical Society backyard, and find it a nobler place at Gay Head, overlooking the cliffs and the sea and the reefs—where it belongs.

—Katrina Wuerth, Ten Penny Farm, Ashland, Mass.

DCHS president Gerald Chittendon, in early March 1952, stated to the *Boston Globe*:

Our attitude is this—we've been working about a year now on this project. [We have] consulted architects, published plans, collected a considerable sum of money, and let a contract for the housing of the lens. The Dukes County Historical Society, if it is awarded custody of the lens, desires nothing but to preserve if for its historical and scientific interest. It cannot assume responsibility for any exhibit 20 miles from its base here in Edgartown, cared for by either a volunteer or a caretaker paid by any other authority.

In the final analysis, the U.S. Coast Guard decided to transfer the Gay Head Fresnel to the Dukes County Historical Society.

Both sides made strong arguments for their respective positions. However, since time was of the essence to find a safe home for the Fresnel, it seems the Coast Guard chose the DCHS because it had the property, the money, the staffing infrastructure and an understanding of caring for historical artifacts.

Today, the Gay Head Fresnel lens with its 1,008 handmade crystal prisms is valued in excess of $3 million.

CHAPTER 16

ISLAND LIGHTHOUSE TESTIMONY

Lighthouse testimony touched on our island's Tattoo from Moby Dick,
shared our maritime history; the meaning of Gay Head Light to our community

Statement of John F. Bitzer Jr.
Chairman, Vineyard Environmental Research Institute (VERI)
and
William Waterway Marks
Founder/President (VERI)

April 30, 1986 (Serial No. 99-34)
Testimony Before the Subcommittee on Coast Guard and Navigation of
the Ninety-ninth Congress, Second Session on:
"The Job of Preserving and Restoring American Lighthouses for Future
Generations Who Have Interest in Maritime History and the Sea"

Mr. BITZER. *Thank you, Mr. Chairman. I am John Bitzer. I am a
volunteer chairman of the Vineyard Environmental Research Institute.
To my left is William Marks, who is the founder, President, and, really,
Director of the institute.*

*The institute thanks you for the opportunity to make our presentation
today. It is reassuring to many that you have interest in the historical value,
as well as the future of U.S. lighthouses, in general, and of those on the
island of Martha's Vineyard specifically.*

The Vineyard Environmental Research Institute is a nonprofit, tax-exempt institute established for the purpose of performing oceanographic and other environmental research. One aspect of our research is to study the effects of hurricanes, storms, ocean currents, rain, and wind relative to shore erosion rates at Martha's Vineyard. In performing this research our scientists work closely with other scientists at the well-known Woods Hole Oceanographic Institute. In fact, the assistant chairman at Woods Hole is a member of our board of directors.

Vineyard Environmental Research Institute also has staff resources responsible for performing historical research relative to the island of Martha's Vineyard. Such research will add greatly to an accurate historical record of the island's lighthouses.

We thank you again for the opportunity, sir.

Ladies and Gentlemen: We of Vineyard Environmental Research Institute thank you for the opportunity to make this presentation before you today. Your interest in the historical value and maintenance of United States Lighthouses, and of those on the island of Martha's Vineyard specifically, is reassuring

The value of a lighthouse to an island people and the rest of America extends far beyond its important purpose of saving ships and lives. When we speak of our lighthouses we also speak of early American history, art, romanticism, folklore, and literature. These are the very things by which a people as a nation trace their early beginnings from our forefathers.

And too, as we have learned, the modern-day cost of replacing a lighthouse can be expensive—as in the recent case history of Nantucket's Great Point Lighthouse, which was recently washed into the ocean and is now, as I speak before you, being reconstructed at a cost in excess of $1 million.

The history of the lighthouses on Martha's Vineyard dates back to the Eighteenth Century. At that time, in 1798, a Lighthouse Appropriations Bill was submitted to Congress, which included the funding of $5,750 for Martha's Vineyard's first lighthouse. At that time, there were fewer than twenty lighthouses operating in the United States. It is of interest to note that these first lighthouses used whale oil as a fuel source. And, as we know from history, Martha's Vineyard's whaling fleet was one of the country's most important sources of whale oil. Need I remind you that Herman Melville, our famous U.S. novelist, poet, and author of Moby Dick, *had many ties to the Island of Martha's Vineyard during its whaling and shipping days.*

Additional history significant to Martha's Vineyard and our U.S. Congress is that during the War of 1812, Congress hired Winslow Lewis to install his improved lighting systems on all U.S. lighthouses, and our Martha's Vineyard lighthouse was the first to receive this new system. Also, in a congressional report published in 1852, the only lighthouse existing on Martha's Vineyard at that time was ranked 9th on a listing of the most important seacoast lights in the United States. At the present time, there are five lighthouses on Martha's Vineyard.

After a physical evaluation of these lighthouses by our Institute's President, we are pleased to report that the overall condition of the Vineyard's lighthouses is relatively good when considering their age; however, due to vandalism and neglect over time, each of these lighthouses will require a significant investment for repair and yearly maintenance.

The primary goal of any U.S. lighthouse management policy should be to ensure the maintenance of these structures as aids to navigation. The leasing or licensing of lighthouses to appropriate local groups is one cost-effective way to meet this goal. Also, the element of local pride and purpose will stimulate the communities involved to undertake programs to protect, repair, and maintain their lighthouses far into the future.

On Martha's Vineyard, Vineyard Environmental Research Institute is a nonprofit, tax-exempt Institute established for the main purpose of performing oceanographic research. One aspect of this research is to study the effects of hurricanes, storms, ocean currents, rain, and wind relative to the erosion rates of our island. In performing this research, our scientists work closely with other scientists at the well-known Woods Hole Oceanographic Institute. In fact, the assistant Chairman of Research at Woods Hole is a member of our Board of Directors.

Vineyard Environmental Research Institute also has a staff responsible for performing historical research relative to the Island of Martha's Vineyard. We feel this research staff will add greatly to creating an historical record of the Island's lighthouses.

At present, Vineyard Environmental Research Institute is working with the 1st Coast Guard District to implement a program to preserve, protect, and maintain the lighthouses on Martha's Vineyard. In doing so, our Institute will help preserve the historicity of our local lighthouses while also utilizing them for the purpose of scientific research. By studying erosion rates from several key lighthouse locations, our Institute will be contributing to a newly evolving base of scientific knowledge about forecasting coastal erosion rates on Martha's Vineyard and the United States' Eastern Seaboard.

Besides repairing the lighthouses and protecting them from vandalism, the Institute's measurement and forecasting of erosion rates near the lighthouses will further assist the Coast Guard's effort in preserving the integrity of these tangible sentinels of early American history.

Thank you.

Mr. STUDDS. *Thank you, sir. Mr. Bitzer, Mr. Marks, did you leave Martha's Vineyard in order to come to Washington for this purpose?*

Mr. BITZER. *William did, sir. I am a summer resident and taxpayer of the Vineyard; I came down from Pittsburgh.*

Mr. STUDDS. *That is arguable—what Mr. Marks did is downright irrational. I apologize for making you do that. We will be on the Island in a couple of weeks. Have your relationships with the Coast Guard been at all adversely affected by the decision of the islands to secede from the United States a few years ago?* [laughter]

Mr. BITZER. *Not that we are aware of.*

Mr. STUDDS. *That's good. Let me ask you, sir; I received a letter from the Coast Guard last month that said that a draft of a license with your organization is currently pending approval in the 1ˢᵗ Coast Guard District for Gay Head Light, Edgartown Light, and East Chop Light. According to that letter, which I received 6 weeks ago, your license was expected to be approved within a month. The first question is the obvious one. Has it been approved?*

Mr. MARKS. *No it has not, Mr. Studds.*

Mr. STUDDS. *Well, that certainly gives us a question for the Coast Guard. What is the intended duration of the license?*

Mr. MARKS. *The intended duration of the license will be 5 years initially, and an additional 30 years subsequent to that. Perhaps you are aware of the fact that this is the first license issued by the 1ˢᵗ Coast Guard District. So they are handling it this way in the beginning.*

Mr. STUDDS. *On what sources of funding does your organization depend?*

Mr. MARKS. *We have a very substantial board of directors. We have a membership as well as quite a few people who are involved in benefit-raising with us. On the Vineyard, as you know, we have quite a bit of talent.*

Mr. STUDDS. *Yes, I know that. When was the organization created?*

Mr. MARKS. *Three and a half years ago.*

Mr. STUDDS. *Do you anticipate at this point—I should have asked you this with the first question—any problems with your license approval?*

Mr. MARKS. At this time we do not. It has been very fruitful and educational dealing with the 1ˢᵗ Coast Guard District relative to this subject.

Mr. STUDDS. So at this point, as far as you know, it is simply a question of your interpretation of a month versus their interpretation of a month? [laughter]

Mr. MARKS. Yes sir.

Mr. STUDDS. I know that the Coast Guard has agreed to go ahead and move Cape Pogue Light as a result of the erosion problem there. Do you know the exact status of that project, and when the work is likely to be done?

Mr. MARKS. The work is due to be initiated within the next 3 to 4 months. As you know, it is…

Mr. STUDDS. Are those Vineyard months or Coast Guard months?

Mr. MARKS. I believe they are Coast Guard months.

Mr. STUDDS. I see.

Mr. MARKS. Yes. [laughter]

Mr. STUDDS. Go ahead.

Mr. MARKS. As you know, that lighthouse is in a very precarious situation. It will only take one good winter storm or hurricane this late fall and it will be gone.

Mr. STUDDS. That is right. So it might be important to do that in Vineyard months.

Mr. MARKS. Yes, hopefully, if you can help.

Mr. STUDDS. We will do our best. Under your agreement to lease lighthouses on the Vineyard from the Coast Guard, to what extent will you be responsible for the maintenance of the properties?

Mr. MARKS. We will be fully responsible for the maintenance of the structure. As far as the aid to navigation is concerned, that will remain with the Coast Guard.

Mr. STUDDS. What sort of research do you plan to conduct on those properties? Anything other than the actual erosion itself?

Mr. MARKS. And the basic ecology that exists there. Our intention is to maintain it as is.

Mr. STUDDS. That is great. I appreciate that, and I appreciate the enthusiasm and the good news that your organization brings to bear on the subject. Go back to the Vineyard immediately; do not pause for any reason in this city. Go home. You won't like it here. Has spring come to the island yet?

Mr. MARKS. No.

Mr. STUDDS. I didn't think so.

Mr. MARKS. But your advice is well taken.

Mr. STUDDS. I know that. [laughter] *The thing is that you know that it will, and that soon it won't require a magnifying glass to establish that it is imminent. That is very good. Thank you all for your testimony. I appreciate it very much.*

We go to the final panel, which I gather consists of the Coast Guard. And if you want to hang around for 5 minutes you might find the answer to your question about the length of a Coast Guard month.

Rear Adm. Kenneth Wiman, Chief of the Office of Engineering of the Coast Guard, accompanied by Capt. William Brogdon. Admiral Wiman, welcome.

For the record: VERI's thirty-five-year lighthouse license was the first in U.S. history whereby a civilian organization assumed control of "active" aids to navigation from the United States of America. It was also the first time in island history that a Vineyard organization assumed control of island lighthouses.

As the founder of VERI, in 1983, I initiated the effort to save three endangered island lighthouses from possibly being razed and replaced with steel towers and strobe lights. In 1986, the U.S. Coast Guard licensed the Gay Head, East Chop and Edgartown lights to VERI. After ten years as president of VERI, I transferred the three lighthouses to the Martha's Vineyard Museum in 1994. As a board member of the Martha's Vineyard Museum, I became the first chair of the museum's Lighthouse Committee.

CHAPTER 17

THE FUTURE

In 2013, a "Notice of Availability" was published for the auction of Gay Head Light. Shortly afterward, the light was designated as one of America's most endangered historic places. *Lighthouse Digest* also placed Gay Head Light on its "Doomsday List" of endangered lights.

In 2013, the town of Aquinnah appointed a Save the Gay Head Light Committee to raise funds, explore ownership of the lighthouse and study relocation of the light away from the eroding cliff.

In 2014, the town of Aquinnah applied for ownership of Gay Head Light.

As of this writing, the National Park Service is reviewing the town's application of ownership and its proposed plans for relocating the light. The final outcome will be determined by the U.S. Secretary of the Interior.

AFTERWORD

Among the tens of thousands of lighthouse aficionados around the world, the Gay Head Lighthouse ranks high in the standings as one of the most beloved and recognizable lighthouses in the United States.

Built on one of the most dramatic and picturesque locations on the East Coast, the lighthouse is considered a "must visit" among the throngs of people who have visited Martha's Vineyard for nearly two hundred years. The fact that it is located on an island has not lessened the desire of lighthouse fans—and others—to make the trek to Martha's Vineyard to visit the magnificent lighthouse and take in its majestic view.

But to the true lighthouse lover, the Gay Head Lighthouse is more than just a pretty location. It is a testament to the early maritime history of our nation and to the lighthouse families who once kept the light, often times under great hardship and loss of life, in unselfish service for the safety of the mariner at sea. Its varied history intertwines with the early development of our country and reflects the economic and historic cultural strength of our nation.

In its prime, the Gay Head Lighthouse with its gigantic first-order Fresnel lens, which was originally displayed at the 1855 World's Fair in Paris, was one of the most powerful and important on the East Coast of the United States. Although the keeper's house has been lost, many of the memories, stories and photographs of life at the lighthouse continue to fascinate people.

Today, this steadfast tower, which was built for one purpose only—to save lives—continues to stand proudly alone, void of human life, sending out its warning beacon to save the lives of those at sea. Now that it's on *Lighthouse Digest*'s "Doomsday List of Endangered Lighthouses," it's our turn to save the lighthouse.

TIMOTHY HARRISON
Founding publisher/editor, *Lighthouse Digest*

List of Gay Head Light Keepers: 1799 to Present

W hat follows is a current list of Gay Head Light keepers. It is my hope that other deserving keepers will be discovered and added.

Ebenezer Skiff (principal keeper, 1799–1828)
Ellis Skiff (principal keeper, 1828–45)
Samuel H. Flanders (principal keeper, 1845–49 and 1853–61)
Henry Robinson (principal keeper, 1849–53)
Ichabod Norton Luce (principal keeper, 1861–64)
Calvin C. Adams (principal keeper, 1864–68)
James O. Lumbert (principal keeper, 1868–69)
Horatio N.T. Pease (assistant keeper 1863–69; principal keeper 1869–90)
Frederick H. Lambert (assistant keeper, circa 1870–72)
Calvin M. Adams (assistant keeper, circa 1872–80)
Frederick Poole (assistant keeper, circa 1880–84)
Crosby L. Crocker (assistant keeper, circa 1885–92)
William Atchison (principal keeper, 1890–91)
Edward P. Lowe (principal keeper, 1891–92)
Crosby L. Crocker (principal keeper, 1892—1920)
Leonard Vanderhoop (assistant keeper, 1892–94)
Alonzo D. Fisher, Crosby Crocker's son-in-law (assistant keeper, 1894–?)
William A. Howland, (assistant keeper, 1897–?)
Charles Wood Vanderhoop (principal keeper, 1920–33)

During the winter, keepers rubbed glycol antifreeze on the exterior glass to prevent ice and snow from blocking the light's signal. In this circa 1875 photo, the lighthouse bricks appear whitewashed. *Martha's Vineyard Museum.*

Max Attaquin (assistant keeper, 1920–33)
James E. Dolby (principal keeper, 1933–37)
Frank A. Grieder (principal keeper, 1937–48)
Sam Fuller (assistant keeper, circa 1940s)
Arthur Bettencourt (principal keeper, 1948–50)
Joseph Hindley (principal keeper, 1950–56)
William Waterway Marks (principal keeper, 1985–94)
Charles Vanderhoop, Jr. (assistant keeper, 1985–90)

Gay Head Light's current double-barrel white-and-red signal was installed in 1988.
Author's collection.

Helen Manning (assistant keeper, 1985–90)

Robert McMahon (assistant keeper, 1985–90)

Richard Skidmore and Joan LeLacheur (assistant keepers, 1990–94; principal keepers 1994–present)

GAY HEAD LIGHT TIMELINE

1789	The U.S. Lighthouse Establishment is created by the Ninth Act of Congress.
1796	Massachusetts state senator Peleg Coffin requests a lighthouse for the Gay Head Cliffs overlooking Devil's Bridge and Cuttyhunk's Sow and Pigs Reef.
1798	Funding for lighthouse is approved by Congress.
1799	On July 1, President John Quincy Adams signs proclamation entitled "Withdrawal of Land at Martha's Vineyard, Massachusetts for a Lighthouse."
1799	An octagonal wooden lighthouse is built on west end of Martha's Vineyard in the town of Gay Head. On November 18, Gay Head Light's first keeper, Ebenezer Skiff, lights the whale oil spider lamps that emit an intermittent "white flash" signal.
1812	Lighthouse receives new light consisting of ten Lewis lamps with fourteen-inch reflectors; Lewis lamps were more labor intensive but maintained the "white flash" signal.
1823	Cuttyhunk Lighthouse built on Cuttyhunk Island's west end—emits "fixed white" signal; Gay Head Light and Cuttyhunk Light mark hazards and both sides of the opening to Vineyard Sound.
1837	The top of the lighthouse is replaced, as there was considerable rot damage to the wooden structure and the lantern and railing areas were very rusted; the light was out while the work was being done.

1838	Ten parabolic lenses installed at Gay Head Light during the summer; lantern lowered fourteen feet. In theory, this was to allow the light to project beneath the layers of fog.
1841	The first Fresnel lens in a United States lighthouse is imported from France and installed in Navesink Lighthouse in New Jersey. A first-order Fresnel lens is installed in the Navesink north tower, and the revolving second-order Fresnel lens is installed in the south tower.
1844	Gay Head Light is moved back seventy-five feet from the edge of eroding cliffs.
1850	Sankaty Head Lighthouse is built on Nantucket; receives second second-order Fresnel lens to be installed on a U.S. light.
1852	Gay Head Light receives new lighting room with large plate glass; Lewis lamps replaced by thirteen new lamps with largest-sized reflectors. U.S. Lighthouse Board takes over control of all lights and organizes country into twelve lighthouse districts, with the Gay Head Light in the Second District.
1854	U.S. Congress approves purchase of a first-order Fresnel to be installed atop a new brick tower.
1855	Construction begins on new brick tower and keeper's home at Gay Head Light; new tower to accommodate new first-order Fresnel lens.
1855	Completion of Fresnel by Lepaute Manufacturing; Gay Head Fresnel entered into 1855 World's Fair in Paris and wins a gold medal.
1856	New first-order Fresnel lens installed on a brown cast-iron pedestal at Gay Head Light and activated on December 1. This was the second first-order Fresnel lens to be installed on a U.S. lighthouse. The Fresnel lens installed at Gay Head Light was a greatly improved first-order Fresnel, which is why it won a first-place gold medal at the 1955 World's Fair in Paris. Its initial signal was an intermittent white flash signal.
1857	Wooden lighthouse is auctioned off and disassembled.
1858	Tours of Gay Head Light's Fresnel lens begin in earnest.
1860	All U.S. lighthouses are converted to Fresnel lens systems.
1867	Lighting fuel in all U.S. lights is changed from sperm whale oil to lard oil to reduce costs.
1869	U.S. Lighthouse Service designs the first federal government flag to be flown at U.S. lighthouses. This first flag of the U.S.

Lighthouse Service is a red, white and blue pennant with a lighthouse silhouette.

1874   On May 15, Gay Head Light signal changed from intermittent flashing white to three whites and one red; the brick exterior of the lighthouse is repainted and the barn new silled, shingled and whitewashed.

1879c   Massachusetts Humane Society establishes lifeboat facility at Gay Head and other island beaches.

1880   All U.S. lighthouses are converted to kerosene oil.

1883   Steamboat dock named Ocean Pier is built at Pilot's Landing on the Sound side of the Head, just east of Devil's Bridge.

1884   First uniforms are introduced for male lighthouse keepers (1,600 in number), and the wearing of both dress and fatigue uniforms becomes mandatory; female lighthouse keepers are not required to wear a uniform.

1884   The Pavilion dance hall, a restaurant, a barn and separate sex outhouses are built a short distance from Ocean Pier at Pilot's Landing.

1890   U.S. Signal Service installs telephone on September 25 with wire connection to Cedar Tree Neck and Woods Hole for sending weather and military information to Washington, D.C.

1890c   There is a mysterious series of illnesses and deaths of a Gay Head Light keeper and another keeper's children.

1884   On January 17, the *City of Columbus* wrecks on Devil's Bridge.

1885   The Gay Head Light lamp is converted to burn kerosene for economic reasons.

1885   U.S. Life-Saving Service (USLSS) builds station with tower near Gay Head Light and boathouse on beach near Dogfish Bar; these replace two previous buildings built for similar purposes by the Massachusetts Humane Society.

1885   USLSS issues two sets of uniforms for all lighthouse keepers with instructions for proper use. This is the only time that lighthouse keepers receive free uniforms. All future lighthouse keepers had to purchase or have their uniforms made according to USLSS specifications.

1885   A brick oil-house, eleven by sixteen feet, is built and provided with a lightning conductor.

1892   On March 11, thirty-seven-year-old Leonard Vanderhoop assumes duties as an assistant keeper at Gay Head Light, making him the first Native American to be employed by the U.S. Lighthouse Board. (Source: original handwritten 1892 Gay Head Light keeper's log at Martha's Vineyard Museum).

1893   For annual fee of $500 paid to town of Gay Head, the Gay Head Clay Co. mines an untold number of tons of clay and transports it via steamboat to brick manufacturers in Boston, Somerset, Providence and elsewhere.

1895   The U.S. Coast Guard takes over USLSS station and boat house and renames facility Coast Guard Station Gay Head.

1898   Some historic records report that all seacoast lighthouses were turned off for the first time in history as a precaution during the Spanish-American War. Other historic sources indicate that the lights remained on during the war.

1898   USLSS takes over many Massachusetts Humane Society boathouses and stations.

1899   USLSS inspects brick keeper's house after deaths of Crocker family children.

1900   Three flights of new iron stairs are placed in the tower, and the stairway is enlarged through the three cast-iron decks.

1902   Brick keeper's home is replaced by two-story wooden home. Due to deaths of children and mold and mildew conditions - home declared "too damp and unsanitary for safe occupation by human beings." New wooden keeper's house is built higher off the ground than previous keeper's house and has no porch.

1905c   Josephine (Smalley) Vanderhoop and her second husband open Vanderhoop Restaurant next to lighthouse.

1908c   Keeper's house has porch added with "X" design railing.

1909   Charles W. Vanderhoop Sr. and his brother, Bert, buy Vanderhoop Restaurant from their parents.

1910   An act of Congress abolishes the U.S. Lighthouse Board and creates the Bureau of Lighthouses to be in charge of all lighthouses, thus changing its operating name from the United States Lighthouse Establishment (USLHE) to the United States Lighthouse Service (USHLS).

1911c   Charles W. Vanderhoop Sr. joins the U.S. Life-Saving Service and sells his interest in Vanderhoop Restaurant to his brother, Bert, and his wife.

1912	Lamp at Gay Head Light converted to an incandescent oil vapor (IOV) burner using a two-inch mantle. This state-of-the-art lamp burned kerosene vapor, which produced a more brilliant light from a smaller lamp. This installation was one of the first of its kind in the United States.
1912	Charles W. Vanderhoop Sr. serves as assistant keeper at Sankaty Head Lighthouse on Nantucket for one year.
1914	The completion of the Cape Cod Canal reduces the number of ships sailing through Nantucket Sound and passing Gay Head Light.
1915	An act of Congress merges the Revenue Cutter Service with the U.S. Life Saving Service, creating a single maritime service—the U.S. Coast Guard.
1919–20	Charles Vanderhoop Sr. becomes principal keeper of Sankaty Head Light on Nantucket and is the first Native American in U.S. history to serve in that capacity.
1920–33	Charles Vanderhoop Sr. serves as principal keeper of Gay Head Light.
1923	Rum-running pirates massacre and sink the steamer *John Dwight* in Vineyard Sound. The steamer *Islander*, the first modern car-carrying vessel to Martha's Vineyard, makes its maiden voyage.
1928c	Not-A-Way inn and restaurant built by off-islander from New Bedford named Gennochio; Helen Manning's mother, Evelyn Moss, manages the inn's restaurant for new owners Milton and Thelma Weisberg.
1931	South Road to Gay Head is completed.
1932c	Vanderhoop Restaurant burns down.
1934c	Trucks begin replacing lighthouse tender ships. With improving road system, the U.S. Lighthouse Service begins using motor trucks to supply some lighthouses and other easy to reach shoreline aids to navigation.
1939	The U.S. Coast Guard takes control of all lights—first time in U.S. history that a U.S. military branch of government takes over a civilian branch of government. All U.S. lighthouses and other aid to navigation systems come under control of U.S. military department.
1940c	Napoleon Madison builds Aquinnah Shop and restaurant overlooking clay cliffs.
1941	Gay Head Light dimmed as a war measure; the entire circle and head area is blockaded as a restricted military zone.

1941	Two concrete bunkers (pillboxes) are installed—one to the north of the Gay Head Light and one to the south.
1944	Cuttyhunk Light is heavily damaged by tidal surge of waves during the Great Atlantic Hurricane.
1946	Gay Head Light is restored to full brilliance.
1947	Cuttyhunk Light is deactivated, torn down and replaced with steel skeleton tower with strobe.
1951	Gay Head gets electric lights and the electrification of the island and state is complete.
1951	The U.S. Coast Guard installs square brick lookout tower on the west side of Gay Head Light.
1952	The U.S. Coast Guard moves the Cuttyhunk Coast Guard Station building to Menemsha by barge; U.S. Coast Guard physically abandons the Gay Head Station and its lookout tower building and Dogfish Bar boast house.
1952	Helen Manning builds her home on inherited land abutting Gay Head Light property.
1953	Old Coast Guard Station Gay Head lookout tower building and related buildings are demolished and removed from bluff above Gay Head Cliffs.
1953	Gay Head Light and U.S. Coast Guard tower electrified; Fresnel lens replaced by high-intensity Carlisle & Finch DCB-224 aero beacon; Fresnel lens and clockworks installed in display tower on grounds of Dukes County Historical Society in Edgartown.
1954	U.S. Coast Guard commissions new station at Menemsha and physically abandons Gay Head station; however, station name in Menemsha remains as Coast Guard Station Gay Head.
1956	Keeper Hindley, the last keeper to man the Gay Head Light, and his family leave property; lighthouse is closed to public.
1961–62	U.S. Coast Guard brick lookout tower at Gay Head is razed and debris removed from its location next to Gay Head Lighthouse; top of tower is sold to a nearby property owner for one dollar and converted into a mini guest house.
1962–63	Gay Head Light keeper's house is razed and removed.
1966	The Gay Head Cliffs are designated a National Landmark by the National Park Service.
1974	U.S. Coast Guard changes name of Coast Guard Station Gay Head to Coast Guard Station Menemsha to reflect physical location.

1984	U.S. Coast Guard considers decommissioning three Martha's Vineyard lights: Gay Head Light, Edgartown Harbor Light and East Chop Light.
1986	VERI chairman John F. Bitzer Jr. and VERI president William E. Marks give testimony before congressional committee to transfer via license the three endangered lighthouses to VERI; it is the first time in U.S. history that "active" lights are transferred to a civilian organization.
1986	Three Martha's Vineyard lights are transferred to VERI via license; William E. Marks takes on duties of modern-day principal keeper at Gay Head Light.
1987	The Wampanoag tribe of Gay Head receives federal recognition and jurisdiction over the "face of the clay cliffs."
1988	The aero beacon is replaced by single-tiered, double-cannon high-intensity DCB-224 beacon; signal is changed from "white, white, white and red" to "white and red"; U.S. Coast Guard transfers ownership of aero beacon to VERI, which loans it to Martha's Vineyard Museum for display.
1989	The lighthouse opens to the public on Mother's Day.
1990	Richard Skidmore and Joan LeLacheur are appointed as assistant keepers by William E. Marks.
1994	VERI founder/president William E. Marks transfers licenses of three lights to Dukes County Historical Society (DCHS); Marks, who is also a DCHS board member, is appointed chairman of DCHS's first Lighthouse Committee; Richard Skidmore and Joan LeLacheur assume principal keeper duties.
2005	The Cuttyhunk steel skeleton tower is discontinued and removed.
2013	A "Notice of Availability" is published for auction of Gay Head Light; the town of Aquinnah appoints Save the Gay Head Light Committee to relocate lighthouse away from eroding cliff.
2014	The Town of Aquinnah applies for ownership of Gay Head Light.

Silent Light

other side—through long dark voyage—light
slipping silently between bleak sullen clouds
igniting smoldering crowns of migration
as distant refracted flame leaps into our eyes
revealing mist hovering above clay collage

powerless our witness
as waves thrum in deep resonance
slowly stretching slumbering chords to sing mourning song
to grace our world with patterns of ancient birth rings
gifted by feathers strumming silvery gossamer strings

rising, rising, rising as tidal plain lifts Snowy Owl's eye
to night sky—to touch lonely stars for infinite affirmation

thus dawn composes music to celebrate our landfall
in rhythm and rhyme to embrace our joyful survival;
survival through our persistence to dream
with hope of being blessed by caress of patiently waiting love
to selfishly desire another touch, another sunrise, another sunset
another flock of birds singing—as our feet press into warm shifting sands
we listen to distant laughter of innocent children playing on

tomorrow's edge

ww

BIBLIOGRAPHY

Adamson, Hans Christian. *Keepers of the Lights.* New York: Greenberg, 1955.

Banks, Charles Edward. *The History of Martha's Vineyard, Dukes County, Massachusetts.* Boston: George H. Dean, 1911.

Bartlett, Captain John Russell (U.S. Navy). "Watching for the Enemy in the Spanish War." *Century Illustrated Magazine* 62, 1901.

Clark, Admont G. *Lighthouses of Cape Cod—Martha's Vineyard—Nantucket: Their History and Lore.* Hyannis, MA: Parnassus Imprints, 1992.

D'Entremont, Jeremy. *The Lighthouse Handbook: New England.* Kennebunkport, ME: Cider Mill Press, 2008.

Dukes County Intelligencer, various issues.

Dvorsky, George. "1846: The Year We Hit Peak Sperm Whale Oil." http://io9. com/5930414/1846-the-year-we-hit-peak-sperm-whale-oil.

Ewan, N.R. *Early Brick Making in the Colonies.* Camden: West Jersey Press, 1970.

Gales, Jeff (executive director of the United States Lighthouse Society). Personal interview. October 5, 2010.

Hough, Henry Beetle. *Martha's Vineyard.* Rutland, VT: Academy Books, n.d.

Howe, M.A. DeWolfe. The Humane Society of the Commonwealth of Massachusetts. Cambridge, MA: Riverside Press, 1918.

The Humane Society of the Commonwealth of Massachusetts. http://www. masslifesavingawards.com.

The Keeper's Log (published by the United States Lighthouse Society), various articles.

Kroes, Florence Leonard. "Brickmaking: A History." http://nancykroes.com/ brickyard/history.html.

Lighthouse Digest, various articles.

Lubrano, Annteresa. *The Telegraph: How Technology Innovation Caused Social Change.* London: Routledge, 1997.

Marks, William E. "Benjamin Franklin's Discovery of the Gulf Stream." *Water Encyclopedia.* Hoboken, NJ: John Wiley & Sons Inc., 2005.

———. *The History of Wind-Power on Martha's Vineyard.* New Bedford, MA: National Association of Wind-Power Resources Inc., 1981.

———. *The Holy Order of Water: Healing Earth's Waters and Ourselves.* Great Barrington, MA: Bell Pond Books, 2001.

Martha's Vineyard Museum. http://www.marthasvineyardhistory.org.

Massachusetts Historical Society. http://www.masshist.org.

Nantucket Historical Association. http://www.nha.org.

National Archives

National Park Service. "Instructions to Employees of the Lighthouse Service, 1881." http://www.cr.nps.gov/maritime/keep/keep1881.htm.

———. "National Historic Lighthouse Preservation Act of 2000." July 8, 2010. http://www.nps.gov/history/maritime/nhlpa/nhlpa.htm.

Naval Facilities Engineering Command. "Project Execution Plan for the Installation of Underwater Power Cables to Smith Island, Cape Flattery, and Destruction Island Lighthouses." September 1, 1976. http://oai.dtic.mil/oai/oai?verb=getRecord&metadataPrefix=html&identifier=ADA165750.

Noble, Dennis L. *A Legacy: The United States Life-Saving Service.* Washington, D.C.: USCG Bicentennial Publications, 1987.

———. *Lighthouses & Keepers: The U.S. Lighthouse Service and its Legacy.* Annapolis, MD: Naval Institute Press, 2004.

Pees, Samuel T. "Oil History: Whale Oil." http://www.petroleumhistory.org/OilHistory/pages/Whale/whale.html.

Putnam, George R. *Lighthouses and Lightships of the United States.* Boston: Houghton Mifflin, 1917.

Safford, S. "A View from the Bricks." *Martha's Vineyard Times,* February 7, 2007.

Snow, Edward Rowe. *Famous Lighthouses of America.* New York: Dodd, Mead and Co., 1955.

Starbuck, Alexander. *History of the American Whale Fishery.* Waltham, MA: self-published, 1878.

United States Coast Guard. "U.S. Lifesaving Service." http://www.uscg.mil/tcyorktown/ops/nmlbs/Surf/surf1.asp.

US-Census.org. "Dukes County, MA 1900 U.S. Federal Census." http://us-census.org/pub/usgenweb/census/ma/dukes/1900/ed242-pg204a.txt.

Wikipedia, various articles.

INDEX

ABOUT THE AUTHOR

William Waterway is the founder of Vineyard Environmental Research Institute (VERI), the nonprofit that saved the Gay Head Light during the 1980s. He won a Gold Medal international award for his book *Water Voices from Around the World* and gained international recognition for his books *The Holy Order of Water* and *The History of Wind-Power on Martha's Vineyard*.

He is the founder of *Martha's Vineyard Magazine*, *Nantucket Magazine* and Martha's Vineyard Poetry Society and the producer of MVTV program series for which he was awarded grants by the Massachusetts Cultural Council. His writings and water research have been featured on TV talk shows and documentary films such as *Acid Rain* (CNN) and *FLOW: For Love of Water*. His work has also been featured in/on *National Geographic*; *Lighthouse Digest*; *The Keeper's Log*; CNN; MSNBC; MVTV; CBS; NBC; ABC; UPI; AP; *New York Times*; *New York Post*; *Newark Star-Ledger*; *Science of Mind*; Coast-to-Coast Radio; *Martha's Vineyard Gazette*; National Public Radio; New Zealand National Radio; the *Water Encyclopedia* (John Wiley & Sons); *Water Consciousness* and *Water Matters* (Alternet); *Transformation: Essays on Love Healing and Water* (Soul Based Living); *Martha's Vineyard Times*; *Cleaveland House Poets*; *An Anthology of Vineyard Poets*; *FDU Magazine*; Care2. com; *Avalon*; *MaximsNews*; and more.

Visit him at www.williamwaterway.com.